In the Spirit

Thanks for speaking
about your chicken stew
making at the Chicken &
Egg Festival. We at the
Alabama Folklife Association
loved it.

Joyce Cauthen
Buf Allen
Sylvia Stephens
11 April 2010

In the Spirit: Alabama's Sacred Music Traditions

Edited by Henry Willett
Director
Alabama Center for Traditional Culture

for the Alabama Folklife Association

In the Spirit: Alabama's Sacred Music Traditions

Edited by Henry Willett
Director
Alabama Center for Traditional Culture
410 North Hull Street
Montgomery, AL 36104

© 1995 by the Alabama Folklife Association
All Rights Reserved

ISBN 1-881320-54-5

ON THE COVER:

Ramah Baptist Church near Letohatchee, Alabama, was established in 1868. First housed in a brush arbor, then a log cabin, the congregation moved into the current structure when it was completed in 1904. Elder Leo King pastors the church today. (Photo by Anne Kimzey)

In memory of

Brenda McCallum

Contents

Acknowledgments

This book is part of a larger project which includes an anthology CD recording of Alabama's sacred music, and a two-day performance festival at the Gadsden amphitheater. The project received grant support from the Folk and Traditional Arts Program of the National Endowment for the Arts, the Lila Wallace–Reader's Digest Community Folklife Program, and the Alabama State Council on the Arts. The project was further supported by a generous gift from Anton Haardt "in memory of Zora Bell Ellis, the woman who raised me, for promotion and support of shape note and gospel music in Alabama."

The title "In the Spirit" was inspired by the title of a documentary radio series produced by the late Brenda McCallum in 1983. This effort is dedicated to her memory.

Introduction

HENRY WILLETT

For some two hundred years, communities and congregations from Athens to Mobile have created, nurtured and sustained a variety of sturdy and joyful sacred music tradtions of immense beauty and power. Folklorists and ethnomusicologists have long recognized Alabama's sacred music traditions as among the state's most remarkable cultural jewels.

Alabama's settlement in the early nineteenth century followed closely the spread of religious revivalism, known as the "Great Revival" or "Second Great Awakening," that swept across the South in that period. The movement, initiated by Tennessee preacher James McGready's fiery sermons on a second Pentecost, brought to Alabama, through tent meeting services, evangelical Protestantism, particularly among Baptists and Methodists.

This religious fervor renewed interest in sacred song. Dozens of songbooks, such as *Kentucky Harmony, Union Harmony* and *Southern Harmony*, were published, and found widespread popularity at religious gatherings throughout the state. The sacred music repertoire of this period (1800-1850) was comprised mainly of psalms, hymns and spirituals. The second half of the century (1850-1900) saw the spread of shape-note singing, particularly from *The Sacred Harp*, across Alabama. The twentieth century brought the explosion of gospel music, in its many forms, with Alabamians playing major roles in the development of those musical styles.

Antebellum Alabamians sang the psalms and hymns of sixteenth and seventeenth century British composers and eighteenth and nineteenth century American composers. This period also witnessed the development of African-American spirituals.

Events of history and culture combined to produce a unique musical tradition in Selma – an African-American congregation preserving a music tradition with direct links to the psalmody of sixteenth century Scotland. The Reformed Presbyterian Church maintains a four-hundred-year-old music tradition, holding to the belief, based upon Biblical directive, that unaccompanied singing of texts from the Book of Psalms is the only proper way to sing God's praise.

Other Alabama congregations have preserved sacred music traditions with origins in the religious music of Africa. Spirituals, first recognized in the early nineteenth century, retain African emphases on vocal embellishment, strong rhythmic qualities, hand-clapping percussion, improvisation and call-and-response.

An antecedent to spirituals, "moaning," is regularly practiced in a number of African-American churches in Alabama. During Sunday devotional service at Spring Hill Baptist Church in Macon County's Cotton Valley, or at any one of scores of other churches across Alabama, the moving and plaintive sound of moaning can be heard. Moaning is often a part of, or interspersed with, the lined-out singing of "Dr. Watts" hymns.

"Lining out," more than likely evolving as a practical solution to a lack of hymn books and literacy in both white and black churches, is where a song leader sings or reads two lines of a hymn, the congregation then repeating the lines in song. "Dr. Watts" refers specifically to the English composer Isaac Watts; though, in fact, refers to any hymns sung in that particular style.

Typically written to be sung in simple meter (common meter, long meter, short meter, etc.), Alabama's African-American "Dr. Watts" adherants sing the hymns with abundant melismatic adornment, counter-rhythm and improvised harmony. The effect is successive waves of vocalization climbing one over the other.

A very different style of hymn singing is found in those Sacred Harp singings of which some three hundred occur in Alabama every year. Taking its name from the songbook *The Sacred Harp*, first published in Hamilton, Georgia, in 1844, this style of singing predates the actual publication of the book. By the eighteenth century religious songbooks were commonly employing shape-notes to indicate the sounds on the then-popular English musical scale fa-sol-la-fa-sol-la-mi-fa. From the fuguing tunes of William Billings to the popular melodies of Jeremiah Ingalls, religious songs found widespread circulation in shape-note hymn books such as *Southern Harmony* and *Social Harp*. It was in this setting that *The Sacred Harp* made its appearance in Alabama in the mid-nineteenth century.

Taught by singing school masters to first sing the notes and then the lyrics, that practice remains to this day a defining characteristic of this *a cappella* tradition. Another defining characteristic is the practice of forming "the square" — basses, tenors, trebles and altos all facing one another.

Typically associated with white culture in the Deep South, southeast Alabama has, nevertheless, enjoyed a vibrant African-American Sacred Harp tradition for well over a century. Alabama slaves might have sung Sacred Harp with whites as early as the 1850s, establishing segregated singings and conventions after the Civil War.

The exceptional durability of Alabama's Sacred Harp tradition is no doubt the result of the strong dedication of a number of extended families — the Woottens of north Alabama's Sand Mountain and the Jacksons of southeast Alabama's Wiregrass region — who have taken on the responsibility of keepers of this cultural tradition.

Similarly, the Deason family, of Bibb and Tuscaloosa Counties, has played a key role in the nurturing of another important Alabama shape-note tradition, Christian Harmony. First published by William Walker, who earlier had published the four-shape *Southern Harmony*, *Christian Harmony*, published in 1866, employed the "modern" seven character note system do-re-mi-fa-sol-la-ti-do. It also contained a number of newer, more contemporary compositions.

There was a time when the two traditions competed for followers, and, in the end, *The Sacred Harp* won many more supporters. But, as witnessed in the annual Capitol City Shape-Note Singing, where both four-shape and seven-shape songs are sung, there are now a number of singers who participate in and support Sacred Harp singings *and* Christian Harmony singings.

While the early twentieth century brought the "Golden Age" of Sacred Harp singing in Alabama, it also brought a new style of sacred music – gospel.

The roots of gospel music can be traced to the emergence of camp meeting songs, revival music, and the incorporation of various styles of secular popular music in the religious songbooks of increasingly sophisticated music publishers. The James D. Vaughan Publishing Company, founded in Lawrenceburg, Tennessee, in 1903, issued one or two new paperback songbooks a year, and, by 1912, was averaging sales of nearly 100,000 books annually.

These books, printed in seven-shape notation, contained mostly new material with about 25 percent of the pages reserved for standards and old favorites. To help promote and market the books, Vaughan created a music institute in Lawrenceburg, where dozens of Vaughan quartets were trained and then sent out to Alabama and across the South to organize singing conventions, to teach singing schools, and, of course, to sell songbooks. Vaughan soon had competitors, most notably from the Dallas-based Stamps-Baxter Music and Printing Company, with its theme song "Give the World A Smile Each Day."

The direct result of the publishing activity of Vaughan, Stamps-Baxter and others are the dozens of community gospel singing conventions, both white and black, found throughout Alabama. The indirect result is the profound impact on the development of a whole variety of gospel styles.

C.A. Tindley, considered by music historians to be the true "father" of African-American gospel, was composing gospel songs during the first decade of the twentieth century; but, it was Georgian Thomas A. Dorsey, composer of such standards as "There Will Be Peace In The Valley," who became the giant of black gospel in the 1930s.

A certain combustion of sacred music styles, fueled by African-American migration from Black Belt tenant farms to the mining and mill towns of Birmingham gave birth to a unique gospel sound. The development of Jefferson County's *a cappella* gospel quartet singing tradition, beginning in the first quarter of the twentieth century, gave rise to the "Birmingham sound," an important and enduring contribution to American gospel music.

Combining the rich harmonies of the various university jubilee singing groups (Fisk, Hampton, Tuskegee) with the style of Vaughan quartets and elements of jazz and ragtime, the Jefferson County quartets discovered a vital new sound characterized by precise, snappy timing and harmonies, a preaching style of lead singing, the trading off of voice parts and a distinctive, percussive "pumping" bass.

Early quartets – the Foster Singers, the Dunham Jubilee Singers, the Famous Blue Jay Singers, the Heavenly Gospel Singers and the Sterling Jubilees, under the tutelage of extraordinarily talented quartet trainers such as Son Dunham and Charles Bridges, set a standard of excellence for other quartets to follow.

Through recordings, radio programs and live performances, the "Birmingham sound" was exported to other cities, further influencing other singers and performers. And just as the early quartets had borrowed from popular, secular music styles, popular performers borrowed from the gospel quartets. The sounds of the Mills Brothers, the Ink Spots, the Platters, Sam Cooke, the Temptations and Boyz II Men are all legacies of the "Birmingham sound."

A number of Birmingham's older gospel quartets are still active. The Sterling Jubilees, the Four Eagles and other groups have maintained the tradition's standards of excellence while inspiring younger groups, like the Birmingham Sunlights, who are bringing fresh innovations to the music while remaining true to the tradition's heritage.

The small town of St. Stephens, in southwest Alabama, has, in recent years, earned a reputation as the center for the promotion of a different kind of gospel sound – bluegrass gospel. Bluegrass, as a popular musical form, incorporates Southern string band music with elements of jazz, blues and gospel. Its vocal style is closely related to the gospel quartet style.

Since Bill Monroe first created bluegrass music in the early 1940s, gospel has been a part of its core repertoire. The Sullivan Family of

Washington County, in their dedication to an exclusively gospel repertoire, have earned the unofficial title "First Family of Bluegrass Gospel Music."

A significant portion of the Sullivans' repertoire is drawn from the gospel compositions of the Louvin Brothers, Charlie and Ira, from the Sand Mountain town of Henagar. This country brother-duet was immensely popular in the 1940s and 1950s, and a number of their songs have become bluegrass gospel standards.

Other bluegrass gospel bands, the Maharreys and Jerry and Tammy Sullivan (both with connections to the Sullivan Family Band) also make the St. Stephens area of Washington County home. All three bands have deep ties to the Holiness-Pentecostal faith. With its relatively unstructured, emotional atmosphere, the Holiness Church accepts a variety of music styles, and warmly embraces the bluegrass gospel of the Sullivans and Maharreys.

Bluegrass gospel adds one more sound to the polyphony of sacred sounds which echo across Alabama: the sound of Luella Hatcher raising the "Dr. Watts" hymn, "A Charge to Keep I Have," at Orrville's Mt. Mariah Primitive Baptist Church; the sound of Japheth Jackson coming to the center of "the square" at the County Line Church in Slocomb, or of Terry Wootten doing the same thing at Antioch Baptist Church in Ider, calling out "page eighty-two," and launching into "Bound for Canaan," a Sacred Harp favorite; the sound of Deacon Tim Menefee of Macon County's Spring Hill Church quietly moaning "Uphill journey but I'm on my way"; the sound of Ernest Phillips as he leads off the monthly meeting of the Lee County Gospel Singing Convention at the Auburn Recreation Center; the sound of John Alexander's Sterling Jubilee Singers performing "God Shall Wipe All Tears Away" at the quartet's sixty-fifth anniversary concert at the Bessemer City auditorium; the sound of song leader Gregory Woodson as he leads Selma's Covenanters in the singing of Psalm 95, "O Come and to Jehovah Sing...." With voices raised, these individuals, and countless others, serve as the keepers of our cultural heritage. In their sacred sounds is the legacy of the Alabama experience.

The African-American Covenanters
of Selma, Alabama

HENRY WILLETT

A recent Sunday found some fifty members of the Selma, Alabama Reformed Presbyterian Church gathering to worship and sing praise from the book of Psalms. Among Alabama's more unique and durable sacred music traditions, this practice dates back to sixteenth-century Scotland. Selma's is the only African-American congregation of the Reformed Presbyterian Church of North America.

On this Sunday morning Pastor Ralph Joseph called out "Psalm 95." Song leader Gregory Woodson and the small choir began the singing, without the aid of musical instruments or a pitch pipe, and the congregation joined in.

> *O come and to Jehovah sing.*
> *Let us our voices raise.*
> *In joyful songs let us the rock*
> *Of our salvation praise.[1]*

The words are from the Book of Psalms, carefully translated so as to maintain the accurate metrical reflections of the Hebrew originals. In this particular singing of Psalm 95, the music is from the old common meter tune, "Alexandria," composed by William Arnold (1768-1832).

Members of the Reformed Presbyterian Church hold to the belief, based upon Biblical directive, that unaccompanied singing of texts from the Psalms is the only proper way to sing God's praise. In sum-

Aimée Shmidt

Reformed Presbyterian Church of Selma.

marizing the church's belief in "exclusive psalmody" the Synod of the Reformed Presbyterian Church of North America has written:

> We believe that God's word clearly sets forth how He is to be worshiped. The reading and exposition of the Word of God are the central focus of our worship. Our musical

praise employs God's word only, thus making use of the divinely inspired Book of Psalms of the Bible. In keeping with the New Testament Church's directive for heart worship, we sing without the aid of musical instruments.[2]

This small Presbyterian sect has congregations scattered throughout Canada and the United States and sister churches of Reformed Presbyterians in Ireland, Scotland and Australia. The origins of the church go back to the sixteenth century claiming early Protestant Reformation leaders Martin Luther, John Calvin and John Knox as spiritual fathers. Reformed Presbyterians are often called "Covenanters," referring to the popular name attached to those who protested the government's establishment of an official state church in seventeenth-century Scotland.

Many early church members signed covenants demanding that control of the Presbyterian Church in Scotland remain in the hands of the presbyteries. King James I responded by launching a savage campaign of executions, ushering in a period that became known as the "killing times." When the "killing times" ended in 1688, all Cov-

Choir of Reformed Presbyterian Church of Selma.

enanter ministers had either been slain or fled the country. The first Reformed Presbyterian Church in North America was organized in 1743.

The origins of the Selma congregation of Covenanters date to the years following the Civil War. The Covenanters had a long history of opposition to slavery, prohibiting the ownership of slaves by its members as early as 1800. In the years immediately preceding the Civil War, Covenanters were active in the Underground Railroad, providing safe harbor for runaway slaves and refusing to comply with the Fugitive Slave Act. After the end of the Civil War a group of Illinois Covenanters traveled to Selma, Alabama, to establish a mission to serve the needs of recently freed African-Americans.

A church and school (Knox Academy) were founded in 1874. The congregation, with twenty-five charter members, erected a church building in 1878. This original building continues in use today.

Psalm-singing, as practiced by the African-American Covenanters of Selma, was once commonplace among various Protestant denominations in the United States. However, beginning around 1800, most denominations gradually turned to the singing of hymns as the preferred form for songs of praise. Only the Reformed Presbyterian Covenanters have strictly maintained their position on exclusive Psalmody. The Covenanters maintain the purity of their Psalm singing, accepting only accurate, metrical translations of the Psalms sung a cappella.[3]

Where the Covenanters are particularly careful with the accuracy of Psalm translations, they feel free to experiment with the music to which the Psalms are sung. Where some Psalms are sung to very ancient tunes, others are sung to contemporary compositions. In a single Sunday service, the Selma Covenanters sang Psalms to tunes ranging from eighteenth century compositions to post-World War II compositions. Some Psalms utilize tunes dating back to the sixteenth century, such as Psalm 100, which is sung to a tune written by composer Louis Bourgeois in 1551. Other tunes are older still, such as "This End is Night," a fifteenth-century English carol used for Psalm 71. Other tunes are much more contemporary, including a number of early 1970s compositions in the Church's most recent edition of *The*

Book of Psalms for Singing.

The precise metrical nature of the Psalm translations requires metrical tunes for their singing. The most frequently found meters are: common meter (four lines of eight, six, eight and six syllables respectively), as in Psalm 95 cited earlier; long meter (four lines of eight syllables each); and short meter (four lines of six, six, eight and six syllables respectively). Less frequently psalms are sung to meters which have no common name, and are labeled simply by the number of syllables per line, as in 88, 88, 88 and 87, 87. Most of the Psalms sung by the Selma Covenanters utilize common meter tunes.

For more than one hundred and twenty years this African-American congregation in Selma, Alabama, has maintained a sacred music tradition dating back to sixteenth-century Scotland. Unique events of history – the seeking of religious freedom and the seeking of personal freedom – combined to create this sturdy and joyful Alabama vocal tradition.

O all ye kingdoms of the earth,
Sing praises unto God;

And Him Who is the Lord of all
With praises do ye laud.
                                    Psalm 68

The Moan-and-Prayer Event in African-American Worship

WILLIE COLLINS

The African slaves who lived in Cotton Valley and Fort Davis, South Macon County, Alabama in the nineteenth century could not invoke their God and spirit by striking a drum with a singular rhythm as in Africa; but they could strike a moan—"Lord Come By Here" or "Come Holy Spirit"—and be consumed not by a Yoruban or Dahomeyan deity, but by Christianity's third Godhead, the Holy Spirit.

Slaves worshiped through prayer and preaching in invisible and visible churches and developed an African-American folk religion. This religion emphasized *feeling* the Holy Spirit and an ideology and world view that constructively adapted them to their conditions of servitude, providing them with hope and faith for that ensuing uphill journey from slavery to freedom and from earth to heaven.

I believe that moaning, because of its low amplitude, was responsive to the musical needs of the invisible church which demanded that the services be undetected. Moaning evolved out of the slaves' social and religious need to behave in a certain way during worship, whether conducted surreptitiously or in the open. In doing so, they developed a sound to accompany that behavior. Hence, the low sound of moaning arose from behavior necessitated by the proscriptions of slavery. Slaves could quietly moan and outwardly express an inward feeling. In all probability, this was the reason for its evolution.

This introspective, yet outwardly expressive sound of an inward feeling brought the congregants to one accord. If the spirit was present, each moan struck in succession by a congregant was like putting sticks of wood on a fire until the church house caught on fire.

Historically, moaning has been widespread among Baptist, United Methodist, the African Methodist Episcpal (AME), and African Methodist Episcopal Zion (AMEZ) denominations. The moaning tradition has remained viable in a number of rural and some urban African-American Baptist churches in Alabama as well as other places.

Because moaning occurs mostly during prayer and sometimes during preaching I have examined the precise relationship of moaning to prayer, and to a lesser extent, to preaching.[1] This genre of African-American music in all probability preceeded the African-American spiritual song and the blues, and forms the basis of their evolution in the history of African-American music.

This study focuses on moans as a specific category and repertoire of sentences, chanted in musical phrases and repeated two to three times to accompany prayer. Humming is often interpolated into the spoken sentence. A typical sentence might be: "It's an uphill journey, but I'm going home."

In most cultures, moaning suggests lamenting over pain or grief. In African-American culture "moaning" can have several meanings: 1) *moaning as humming* - to sing with the lips closed and without articulation of syllables;[2] 2) *moaning as intonational chant* - to intone the words of a sermon; 3) *moaning as mourning* - Newbell Niles Puckett refers to a category of religious songs spoken of as "mourning" songs.[3] (Moaning is differentiated from "mourning" as the state of seeking one's soul's salvation); 4) *moaning as groaning* - groaning is another term for humming;[4] *moaning as a secular type* - the term moan has also been attached to a group of secular songs as well as a blues singing technique. Most informants defined the moan as: 1) a chant; 2) a prayer; and 3) an outward expression of an inward feeling. Reverend Coleman, a member at Spring Hill Baptist Church in Cotton Valley, defined a moan as follows:

> A moan is the sincere prayer to God for a particular thing in the words of a song. It's a form of singing in a prayer.[5]
>
> I have defined the moan as follows: A sacred chant of one

sentence, repeated two or three times, of approximately thirty-second duration with text generally based on personal experience. It is of individual creation, but may occasionally be based on a hymn title or psalm. It is disseminated by oral tradition. Moans are initiated and expressed *a cappella* during a prayer in prayer service, devotion, and occasionally, during the preacher's sermon. A number of these moans may be led successively by one or several individuals during the course of a prayer. Typically, a leader moans most of the sentence and, near the end, the congregation joins in, in degrees, sometimes initially humming then uttering the words with the leader. Moans are of relatively low amplitude as compared with song. They are melodically embellished with melismas, having a unison and heterophonic texture and are usually performed in a slow, sustained manner.[6]

The texts of moans are concerned with the elicitation of the Holy Spirit. For example, "Come Holy Spirit, We Need You Now," "Why Don't You Come In The Building, If You Don't Stay Long," and "Lord, Come By Here" are all directed towards inviting the Spirit. South Macon County consists of a thirty square-mile area bordered by Montgomery County to the west, Bullock County to the south, and Russell County to the east. The land rolls gently with a number of abandoned farm houses that once supported "King Cotton" on rich, sandy soils. A plantation system based on cotton and utilizing, on the average, the labor of ten slaves per farm, was the principal economy of the region.[7] The Town Creek District Association, formed in 1890,[8] encompasses a consortium of nineteen Baptist churches, four in Bullock County, two in the town of Tuskegee, and thirteen in South Macon County.

Two African-American rural Baptist churches—Elizabeth Missionary Baptist Church and Spring Hill Baptist Church—both having their beginnings in the nineteenth century, are the focus of this study. Their congregants are descendants of a slave population which totaled three to four thousand in the 1860s. Unaccompanied congregational singing was the norm until the 1950s when pianos were secured. Church services are held on the first and third Sundays at Spring Hill and second and fourth Sundays at Elizabeth. Revivals, which occur the first Sunday in August at Spring Hill and the fourth week in April and July at Elizabeth, provided an opportunity to hear numerous moans.

Methodist church historian the Reverend Anson West observed the moaning tradition among Methodists in Alabama as early as the 1830s, commenting on an "African-American style of worship."

> The Negroes were impulsive and demonstrative, and were easily moved. A certain sort of ecclesiastical oratory put them in a glow and set them in motion. Swinging and intoning were popular parts of their worship. There was a peculiar swinging of the body and there was a peculiar voicing of sounds the inhibition of which cooled their ardor and marred their happiness. The preacher who would be acceptable to the Negroes in the days of slavery had to understand their desire to toss and intone during divine service, and grant them liberty and indulgence therein. There was among them in their worship a mixture of sighs, moans, and groans which made a peculiar sound, and which was peculiar to them and which it is impossible to embody in words. While they were not cultured in music, they were gifted in singing. Some of them were able in prayer and in exhortation. They were fervent in spirit, serving the Lord.[9]

From the above description and others, it is clear that moaning was practiced during slavery; and although the Reverend West's description documents the tradition as early as 1832, it is likely that moaning existed before that period, perhaps as early as the beginning of the nineteenth century. When asked, "When did they think moaning existed?" most informants pointed to its origins in slavery. Many of them remembered their grandmothers or grandfathers speaking of moaning. Deacon Theodore Samuel recalled his grandmother Mary

Francis Crawford's account as follows:

> And she used to tell us that they couldn't go to church
> and sing like we were singing when I was coming up and
> growing up. She said that they couldn't go out and ex-
> press themselves and they couldn't go out and sing so
> they just– they would just hum a moan to themselves,
> you know because they had to keep it covered up be-
> cause they wouldn't allow you just that freedom to go
> out and start having church. They had to hide to do it.[10]

Spring Hill has one hundred and fifty three members, eight deacons, and four deaconesses. Elizabeth has a membership of seventy,
four deacons, and three deaconesses. The repertory of moans at Spring
Hill and Elizabeth was created, no doubt, in the cotton fields in the
heat of the day, within the cribs of plantations, and during the night
meetings in the thickets of the pine and oak forests of the Alabama
Black Belt.

The moan-and-prayer event consists of several participants: the
prayer-sayers, the congregation, and the moaners. After the last stanza
of the Hymn 100 (Dr. Watts) has been sung, the congregants will
begin the "humming chorus." A deacon or deaconess will initiate a
prayer while the stanza is being hummed; however, the prayer often is
initiated during humming so that the humming co-occurs with the
prayer. Following the humming chorus, a succession of moans occurs.

In August of 1992, the following moan-and-prayer event occurred
during the devotional part of a revival service at Spring Hill. First, a
congregational song entitled "In My Heart" was sung followed by a
lined-out Hymn 100, "A Charge to Keep I Have." The last chorus
hummed. Then a prayer-sayer began a prayer and successive
moans[11]continued throughout. After the first prayer-sayer completed
his prayer, a second prayer-sayer began praying and a succession of
moans continued to the end of the prayer when the moan-and-prayer
event ended. This example gives only a sketch of the sequence of
occurrences in the moan-and-prayer event. Group participation with

successive moans by different congregants is of high priority at both the Elizabeth and Spring Hill churches. The late Sister Horton of Elizabeth commented on the high point of the moan and prayer event when she stated: "What make it good, you see is that—she'll strike out on one, she'll get through with hers, then another old lady over there, she'll strike out on another and then one over yonder strike off on another. I'm telling you, it sounds good to me..."[12]

As a participant observer, it was demonstrated to me repeatedly that the fire and intensity of "the Spirit" were achieved through the moan-and-prayer event. As the prayer-sayer talked to Jesus through speech, intonational chant, and sometimes chant, the congregants talked back and answered, moaning for Jesus to "come on in the building, if You don't stay long."

Although moaning is considerably different from the spiritual, a number of spirituals mention moaning and groaning in their song texts. One such spiritual, "If You Feel Like Moaning," is sung at Spring Hill. One stanza is:

If you feel like moaning, it ain't nothing but love
If you feel like moaning, it ain't nothing but love
If you feel like moaning, it ain't nothing but love
Ain't Nothing but the fire, coming up from above.[13]

Generally, informants feel that moaning should be "low" – meaning soft in amplitude. "Moaning is just a little old low harmony in your voice that you using and with it, you using it in a low mellow sound."

Moaning has several effects on prayer. Of utmost importance is moaning supporting the prayer-sayer. In response to the question of why one moans during a prayer, informants replied that it was to lend support. Moaning supports the prayer-sayer in the following ways: 1) it enables the prayer-sayer to pray longer; 2) to pray louder; 3) it gives confidence to a young novice or inexperienced prayer-sayer; and 4) it excites the congregants and gains their attention.

It is no longer necessary to hide or steal away to moan; yet the tradition has continued. The uses for the moan and the context of the moan changed with the transformation of the political and legal status of slaves; yet it endured in its function to elicit the spirit, to convert sinners, to infuse spirit, to arouse the attention of the congregants in the devotional service and prayer meetings, and to "shake up the minister" (i.e., urge the preacher on) during sermons. "Tradition is something another; you know it?—when the people got tradition—it's hard to get it out of them—some of it you ain't gonna never get it out of them,"[14]insisted the late Deacon Timothy Menefee in commenting on the resiliency of the moaning practice. This music (moaning) also has resisted change because it has been associated mainly with prayer in the devotional part of the liturgy. Individual improvisation gives a distinct melodic flavor and identity to each moaner.

Moaning is a participatory practice which assists in livening up a dead church. The frequency of the moan-and-prayer and moan- and-sermon event may diminish in frequency as ministers become formally educated or support the discontinuation of the devotion as a prelude to regular worship service. Stagnant economies continue to drain the younger rural population as it migrates to the cities for employment. These factors, along with the older age of most moaners, seriously threaten the continued practice of the moan-and- prayer and moan-and-sermon events in a number of churches.

Moans and groans have transported the African-American Christian from slavery to freedom and from earth to heaven. The moan may be the agent for inducing trance for the spiritual transcendence of the slaves and freed African-Americans serving to convert the sinner, elicit the Holy Spirit, giving vent to built-up tensions and resolutions and freedom from earthly cares and troubles. Moaning is also a medium for communicating the "let's church" drama which is emulated, at an early age, by children playing church, becoming a conditioned reflex, socially contagious, spreading from one believer to the next. This communication over the years has created an insular, stable, and highly valued musical culture. The practice of successive individualized moans, co-occurring with the prayer-and-sermon event, has utilized the value of group participation and freedom of expression. The tradition of the moan-and-prayer event still rests on the experiences of present day life

— that is, being black in America. As Reverend Curry, Sr. of Spring Hill stated:

> Sometimes moaning is agony, sometimes moaning is looking at conditions, you see. Even today, when you see young men, young black brethren destroying themselves with "crack" and various forms of drugs, and when you see white men continuously lay off your brethren and then use them when they are ready to, and then fire them again and hire them back, that makes you moan. See, those things are facts that we have to deal with being concerned Christians, being my concern. I love all people, but my greatest concern is my people.[15]

Moaning evolved out of a particular social and religious need of African-Americans in slavery and has continued because of its usefulness, its pleasing sound, and the efficacy with which moans elicit the Spirit. The African-American Baptist church's "altar call," and "devotion" have enabled the tradition to continue in urban and rural areas. Moaning has remained insular and static, and is a mirror of an older, more vital tradition.

Singing 'Dr. Watts':

A Venerable Hymn Tradition

Among African Americans in Alabama

JOYCE CAUTHEN

From the front of the sanctuary of New Hope Primitive Baptist Church in Eutaw, Alabama, Deacon Smith announces, "We are going to sing 433, 'Lord, in the morning thou shalt hear my voice ascending high.'" Immediately he and the congregation launch into the hymn, repeating the words he has called out in a slow, chant-like song. This time, however, each syllable is meditated upon. The singers hold each for four long beats, embroidering them and giving as much importance to the individual syllables of "as-cend-ing" as to those of "thou shalt hear my voice."

As the congregation sings the last word, Deacon Smith "gives out" the next stanza: "To thee will I direct my prayer, to thee lift up mine eye" and the singers continue their slow, syllable-by-syllable progression through the hymn, unaccompanied by instruments of any sort. Without consulting hymnals, they sing the words that Deacon Smith draws from a small, hard-bound volume entitled *Primitive Hymns*. This little hymnal, which easily rests in the palm of his hand, contains the texts to 700 hymns, without musical notation. Indeed, it is hard to envision these meandering tunes captured upon a musical staff.

Hymns of this style are called "Dr. Watts" by those who sing them in African-American congregations across Alabama. Though they derive their name from English hymnist Isaac Watts, the term refers to the style in which the hymns are sung, rather than their authorship.

Above: New Hope Primitive Baptist Church, Greene County, Alabama.

Left: Road sign to New Hope Primitive Baptist Church, Greene County, Alabama.

Frequently sung "Dr. Watts" hymn, "A Charge to Keep I Have" was actually written by Charles Wesley.

Watts' name was attached to this style of singing because his hymns were in great favor at the time many African-Americans were introduced to Christianity. Born in England in 1674, Watts had begun writing hymns as a young man at a time when only Old-Testament Psalms were sung in Anglican services. Wishing to improve congregational singing, which he observed to be "horrendous and lamentable," Watts composed hymns in simple meter that could be sung to familiar tunes.[1] As was the practice of the day, Watts provided only the poetry, allowing the congregation to sing a particular hymn to any tune with the right number of measures. To aid in selecting an appropriate tune, he provided notations about the meter ("C.M.,"

Aimée Shmidt

Wall decoration, New Hope Primitive Baptist Church, Greene County, Alabama.

"L.M.," "S.M.," etc.)[2] of each hymn. His compositions took into consideration the fact that in most congregations, hymns were "lined out" for those who could not read or did not own hymnals. Thus, he phrased the text in such a way that periodic interruptions by the song leader did not destroy its meaning.[3]

Watts' *Hymns and Spiritual Songs* was published in England in 1707. It became popular in the United States decades later in a period of widespread evangelism known as "the Great Awakening," during which non-Anglican denominations, such as Presbyterians, Baptists, and Methodists, began to proselytize in the South. In the 1750s such men as Samuel Davies of Virginia began ministering to the slave population. Davies, a dynamic Presbyterian preacher and hymnwriter, wrote to benefactors in England requesting materials: "The Books I principally want for them are, *Watts's Psalms and Hymns, and Bibles*...I cannot but observe, that the *Negroes*, above all the Human Species that I ever knew, have an Ear for Musick, and a kind of extatic Delight in *Psalmody*; and there are no books that they learn so soon, or take so much Pleasure in." After receiving them, Davies wrote, "The books were all *very acceptable*; but none more so than the Psalms and Hymns, which enable them to gratify their peculiar taste for Psalmody. Sundry of them have lodged all night in my kitchen; and sometimes, when I have awakened about two or three o'clock in the morning, a torrent of sacred harmony poured into my chamber...In this seraphic exercise, some of them spend almost the whole night." In Davies' services blacks worshipped with whites, but sat in a separate section of the sanctuary. He wrote, "I can hardly express the pleasure it affords me to turn to that part of the Gallery where they sit, and see so many of them with their Psalm or Hymn Books, turning to the part then sung, and assisting their fellows who are beginners, to find the place; and then all breaking out in a torrent of sacred harmony, enough to bear away the whole congregation to heaven."[4]

Many slave owners did not allow slaves to attend church. Those who did permit worship among slaves often required that a white person conduct the services, or at least observe them. To avoid this inhibitive white presence, it was common for slaves to organize "invisible churches," held late at night in secret places. There they sang Watts' hymns as they pleased, in a style that was surely different from what Isaac Watts had in mind when he composed them. And they continued to do so after Emancipation, when they formed visible African-American churches. According to hymn scholar Wendel P. Whalum, "the Black Methodists and Baptists endorsed Watts' hymns, but the Baptists 'blackened' them. They virtually threw out the meter signature and rhythm and before 1875 had begun a new system which, though based on the style of singing coming from England to America in the eighteenth century, was drastically different from it." Whalum describes Dr. Watts singing as having "a rather crudely shaped line which floated melismatically along, being held together primarily by the deacon who raised and lined it."[5] By "melismatically," he meant that the line was composed of a series of melismas, or decorative passages of several notes sung to one syllable of text, as in Gregorian chants.

This approach to hymn singing does away with traditional European melodies. In the liner notes to *Primitive Baptist Hymns of the*

the Blue Ridge, which examine both black and white hymn traditions, music scholar Brett Sutton explains the difficulty of recognizing the melody line of a hymn sung in "Dr. Watts" style:

> The more elaborated a melody becomes, the more it loses the clarity of its contour and the more difficult it is to compare it to the leaner written versions. In the white versions picking out the main notes of the tune is relatively simple and what might be termed the "core" melody is easily derived. But in the black versions, it is not always clear which pitch in the elaborating phrase should be taken as the most important or dominant. Without a way to reduce the phrase to a note the analyst cannot automatically derive a core melody, and any pure melody derived under such difficult circumstances remains somewhat arbitrary.[6]

While ethnomusicologists have terms like those above to explain what is happening musically in Dr. Watts-style hymns, the lay person resorts to words like "strange," "weird," and "eerie." In *A Slave Holder's Daughter,* Belle Kearney, who grew up on an ante-bellum plantation in southwestern Mississippi, used such words to describe the hymn-singing she heard there:

> In the pulpit with the preacher is the precentor— not known by that name—some brother of noted devotional gift who begins the service by "lining out" a hymn, his voice intoning and dimly suggesting the tune with which the congregation follows—one of those wild, weird airs, half chant and dirge, so full of demi-semi-quavers that only the improvisator-soul can divine it, yet so full of strange, sweet melody and pathos, rendered in their marvelously tuneful voices, it is no wonder a suppressed emotion begins to communicate itself through the audience.[7]

Those who have grown up singing Dr. Watts hymns, however, find them simple. They have no trouble grasping where the melody is leading and no trouble distinguishing between the tune of one hymn and another. Elder Vassie Knott, who pastors New Hope Primitive Baptist, says that the tunes are not improvised. A hymn such as "When I Can Read my Title Clear," is sung the same in all the congregations in the Sipsey River Association, to which New Hope belongs. However, in another association or denomination it may sound different. Speaking of the Big Creek Association from Tennessee, Elder Knott said, "You could hear the Sipsey sing and hear them [the Big Creek] sing and you'd wonder how they were Primitives and these are Primitives. I can't sing with them...different beat and everything. They can sing one verse and you can go from here to that filling station. They stretch them out. But they sound good."[8]

The key to singing "Dr. Watts" well is to grow up doing it. Gospel quartet the Poole Brothers, of Tuscaloosa, include powerful, show-stopping renditions of Dr. Watts-style hymns in their performances. Hudson Poole admits that "if they hadn't really been around this hymn singing...if they hadn't been raised around it, it wouldn't sound like nothing. It's something that from childhood you come up with." His brother Andrew adds, "It's hard for people that's been singing for years. I notice people in church—I can hear them cutting off at a certain place. They don't know how to go from there. It needs to be in you. It's got to be brought up in you. You got to know exactly where to carry it."[9] Deacon Walter Lee of Mt. Pleasant Primitive Baptist in Birmingham agrees: "Everybody can't sing it. You got to be raised up with it."[10]

Dr. Watts-style singing is not taught in singing schools; nor do the hymnals contain sections on the rudiments of hymn-singing nor explanations of musical terms. It is still very much an oral tradition, carried on by the deacons, and in rare cases, deaconesses, who "raise," or "give out," the hymns.[11] Some hymn-raisers can lead only a few Dr. Watts hymns; others have sizable repertoires. Elder Knott says that though his church sings a large number of the selections in *Primitive Hymns*, there are many that only a particular deacon can lead. Andrew Poole's father, for instance, knew many hymns that others did not know—hymns which the Poole Brothers wish they could sing today.[12] Deacon Walter Lee of Birmingham is wistful when he thinks of the congregations that have older members who are still good at "that old way of singing...if I had been way on back there singing the hymns, I could sing all those hymns in the way they called them out...But us younger generation...our Pastor says we can't learn all these songs, because we don't have people with the voices to sing them." To build his repertoire of hymns, he takes a tape recorder when he "fellowships" at other churches.

Deacons at both New Hope in Eutaw and Mt. Pleasant in Birmingham raise hymns from *Primitive Hymns*, which was first published in 1841 by Benjamin Lloyd, a white Primitive Baptist minister who arranged and indexed them in such a way that "persons can easily select hymns suited to any occasion of Divine Service."[13] Lloyd lived near Greenville, Alabama, when he published his hymnal which has seen continual use by black and white singers across the nation since its publication.[14] At Mt. Pleasant, the congregation also uses a second hymnal, *The National Primitive Baptist Church Hymn Book*, because some of their favorite hymns, such as "A Charge to Keep I Have," are not in *Primitive Hymns*.

Ownership of hymnals among the congregation is optional. At Mt. Pleasant in Birmingham, most of the congregation bring one or both of the hymnals used there, but at New Hope in Eutaw, few of the members carry them. Elder Knott says they are not needed because all the words are given out. Hymn-raiser Luella Hatcher of Orrville, near Selma, does not own a hymnal but sings, from memory, hymns she learned in childhood. Mrs. Hatcher, a deaconess at Mt. Mariah Primitive Baptist, is allowed to lead hymns because her husband is a deacon there.[15] However, many Primitive Baptist congregations are "hard-shell" or "Old Landmark" churches which follow St. Paul's strictures against women taking a leadership role in worship.[16]

Dr. Watts-style hymns are sung primarily in the opening devotional service, led by deacons before the minister takes the pulpit. In African-American Primitive Baptist churches, and many other old-line

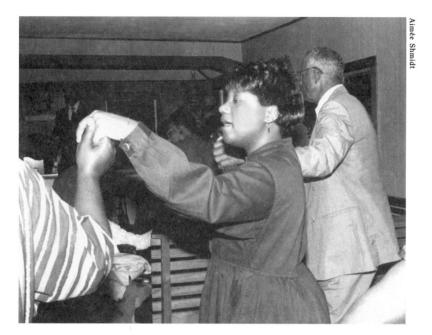

Aimée Shmidt

Joining hands during devotion at New Hope Primitive Baptist Church, Greene County, Alabama.

denominations, the Devotion opens with a Dr. Watts-style hymn, followed by a prayer. During the second "Dr. Watts" members participate in a hand-shaking fellowship ritual with others in attendance. They remain seated during the first verse, but as the second is given out, they rise and walk to any place in the sanctuary where they can extend both hands to others. As they sing the syllables of the two-line stanza, they rotate their arms in time with the music, giving an emphatic double-pulse on the first beat of each four-beat syllable. As the deacon gives out the next two lines they move to another place in the sanctuary and join hands with two more people. This continues throughout as many verses of the hymn as the deacon feels is appropriate. The handshaking is repeated during the next hymn or two, with members trying to reach everyone in the room, aware that this could be the last time they might shake a particular individual's hand. In some churches, the congregation hums the last stanza as individuals return to their seats and prepare for the prayer to follow.

During the handshaking, the congregation cannot use hymnals. Unless they know the hymn by heart, they rely totally on the hymn-raiser and sing exactly the words he gives out. Should he mispronounce a word or skip a line, the congregation will do so as well.

Dr. Watts-style hymns play a crucial role in the Devotion, which is meant to prepare the church-goer for true worship. Andrew Poole says that they "get you in the spirit...get you real serious."[17] Linda Reese, daughter of Deaconess Luella Hatcher, says that Dr. Watts "pushes the devil out...it is a spiritual way of touching everyone in the congregation. The hymns join hearts and minds and get everyone in accord."[18] Deacon Lee explains in colorful analogy:

> Way back in the old days, folks get ready to kill a hog, they don't get out there and kill a hog and then get the water hot. They got to heat the water, sharp the knives, place everything out in order, so when they kill the hog, they got it ready to start cleaning and everything. So its the same way about serving the Lord. You got to turn round and start getting ready for him. And when you wash yourself up and...ask the Lord 'forgive me for my mistakes'..you get in the spirit. You can't sing too much of that hymn, you are ready to start shouting your own self. You are in the spirit.[19]

In Deacon Lee's church, as in many other old-line churches, the Devotion ends as the choir enters to the music of piano and organ. At this point, the singing of "Dr. Watts" is over, unless the minister calls for a hymn in preparation for the sermon. Music for the rest of the service will be "congregational hymns"–spirituals and other familiar, easy to sing hymns–and contemporary gospel numbers led by the choir. However, in the "hard shell" churches of the Sipsey River Association, such as New Hope, pianos, organs, and choirs are not permitted. Dr. Watts-style hymns are sung throughout, with an occasional congregational hymn started by a deacon during a pause in the service. In such churches, seven or eight hymns are sung instead of the two or three sung when "Dr. Watts" is confined to the devotional.

"Dr. Watts" singing and spirituals come to us from a period which Wendel P. Whalum calls "the oral tradition." In this period, beginning with the introduction of slaves to the American colonies, "the manner of dealing with American life as realized by Blacks themselves is hewn, by them, or with little outside help, from a few sources." The oral tradition began to end around 1867 with the presence of schools and strong institutional churches.[20] Over the years, efforts by leaders of some African-American denominations to make their services more relevant, contemporary, or more like Euro-American denominations, have led them to drop the oldest forms of black religious music from their services. Others, however, have revered traditional hymns and spirituals and have ensured their survival. Whalum pays tribute to "the particular group of blacks who prepared and preserved this music:"

> It is this group that insisted, without full endorsement of the clergy, on taking the music from the slave quarter to the institutional church. It is they who, when warned against using this music in the church, found a place for it in prayer meetings, ring shouts, and services as well as in daily personal and community devotions. It is, therefore, to them that we must give the credit for the preservation of the older music types of which we have only a few examples. And, today, isolated in storefront churches, rural towns, and sea islands, they continue to sing the music."[21]

They sing it in Alabama's smallest rural communities and in her largest cities. Like the congregations of the Sipsey River Primitive Baptist Association, they may sing Dr. Watts hymns throughout the service. Or, like the Mt. Pleasant congregation in North Birmingham, they may sing them only during the devotion. But they sing them still—with great respect, reverence, intensity, and skill.

Sand Mountain's Wootten Family: Sacred Harp Singers

BUELL COBB

For the Woottens of northeastern Alabama, the family circle is really a square. To this sturdy clan of shape-note singers, the traditional Sacred Harp formation — a "hollow square" or simply "the square," with each of the four voice parts (tenor, bass, treble and alto) turned in to face the others — is a familiar and cherished structure.

At the churches or homes on and around Sand Mountain where they gather to sing — brothers and sisters, cousins and in-laws, aunts and uncles, grandchildren and great-grandparents — the Woottens make music that is a distillation of their Christian faith and the essence of family unity. The spirit of that singing and the pealing clarity and strength of their *a cappella* sound have stirred the hearts of listeners over the decades and brought the Woottens not only local renown, but also visitors from other Sacred Harp communities from around the country.

Hearing for the first time the Woottens sing — when they are at anything like full strength — is to come upon what seems an almost elemental force. Beyond the power and natural beauty of their individual voices, what compels attention is the purity of their blended sound, an ardent pressing of voices against the discipline of the music they know so well.[1]

Upright and hard-working folk, they are a family closely linked to the land. Though some members have been mill workers and machine-shop operators — a carpenter here, a teacher there — most, for the better part of the century, have been farmers. And though Terry

Wootten, 38, the leader and keyer of music at many of their singing events today, jokingly says that his kin are "scattered like durn sheep," he acknowledges that most live within a 30-mile radius of his home in Ider. The example of Terry, who has taught singing schools in St. Louis, Seattle and even London, is fodder for the observation that usually it is not work or travel for its own sake, but Sacred Harp excursions that lead them far from their home base.

In an interview for Alan Lomax's "American Patchwork" series which aired on public television in 1990, Terry's uncle, the late Chester Wootten, one of the family's premier singers and leaders, spoke of how group singing had been part of the rhythm of daily life for the Woottens of his generation: "We grew up during the Panic, had a hard time living at home. But we would work hard in the field. We'd come in at night, why, we'd all get out on the porch after we eat supper . . . my daddy would start singing. Then we'd start joining in and we'd sing till bedtime. A lot of time, we'd sing till our neighbors would drive in and help us. We'd have a singing before we went to bed."

Sacred Harp singing has been a part of rural Southern life in manifestations similar to the above description for a century and a half. One or another edition of the tunebook *The Sacred Harp* has been in print almost continuously since the original was published in Hamilton, Georgia, in 1844. The genre of shape-note tunebooks — combining folk hymns, fuguing tunes, camp-meeting songs, patriotic songs, odes and anthems — has roots in the New England singing-school movement of the late eighteenth century and the longer tradition of parish psalmody in rural England from up to a century before that. In stretches of the rural South, the Sacred Harp and rival singing traditions — Christian Harmony, Southern Harmony, Social Harp, Harp of Columbia and others (each named for a different tunebook) — claimed great popularity among the folk in the nineteenth and early twentieth centuries. While Sacred Harp, the best known of those traditions, has passed from view and even from memory in many communities, it has survived in others where one or more large, close-knit families have absorbed it as part of their heritage and family identity.

Freeman Wootten holding photo of grandparents Thomas and Rhoda Haynes.

In the modern era, no family has more closely intertwined the lives of its members with the Sacred Harp, or given a more loving account of that relationship, than the Woottens (or, to give credit to the side of the family that claimed the earliest attraction to the singing tradition, the Haynes-Woottens). At work or at leisure, it is often the melodies of the Sacred Harp that keep them company. Most of the family have heard the spirited, richly harmonized music from birth. As infants, in the arms of a mother, grandmother or aunt, they have awakened at innumerable family or community gatherings amid the sound of fifty to a hundred voices at full thrust. Through song after song, they have gazed at the hand and arm motions of relatives on all sides, keeping time as they sang. And, having attained a few years of age, they each have learned to stand before the group themselves and lead a song, beating time in the four-beat style (down-left-right-up) that, until it gained wider popularity through their example, distinguished them from most other traditional Sacred Harp groups. Buoyed by the pride and affection of kin of every side, they are thus initiated into a ritual that bridges the generations.

The time and place at which the family first took up one of the editions of the Sacred Harp book are now probably beyond discovery. But Thomas and Rhoda Haynes must have brought a songbook with them from Georgia when they moved to Alabama toward the end of the nineteenth century, first to Randolph County in central Alabama near the Georgia line, and then to Jackson county near Section, in the northeast corner of the state, where they settled.

A good singer himself, Thomas Haynes taught all fourteen of his children to sing. Like their mother, the eight girls sang treble — by longstanding tradition pronounced "tribble" — the high, wide-ranging harmonic part that helps to distinguish Sacred Harp from other kinds of choral music. The six boys sang either tenor (the melody part) or bass.

Two of the Haynes girls, Beulah and Rhoda, eventually married brothers in their community, Jesse and Charlie Wootten, whose parents had also come from Georgia. Beulah (1884-1967) and Jesse Wootten (1888-1971) in turn had seven children (Gertha, Chester, Postell, Mack, Carnice, Freeman and Olivia), and it is these five brothers and two sisters and their numerous descendants whose names have been so prominently linked with Sacred Harp singing the past few decades. Beulah is said to have taught her husband to sing. As well as acquiring facility at bass and tenor, he learned to sing treble along with her. And when there was a Sacred Harp singing school in the area, the Woottens sent their children for instruction. Freeman Wootten, now seventy-three and Jesse and Beulah's only surviving son, remembers attending his first when he was "just a kid."

The singing schools, which usually lasted about eight hours a day for two weeks, were held during the part of the summer when crops were "laid by." At the schools, the young Woottens and others of their community gained mastery of the shape notes — in the four-shape music tradition of the Sacred Harp, a triangle for Fa (both the key note and the interval of the fourth in the major scale), a circle for Sol (the second and fifth notes), a rectangle for La (the third and sixth), and a diamond for Mi (the seventh or "leading" tone) — and other elements of the system they would need to be able to negotiate their way successfully through any of several hundred songs in the oblong tunebook. In traditional style, they learned to sing each song through once with the shape sounds (thus the moniker "fasola singers") and then with the words.

In time, Jesse and his sons gained a reputation for powerful singing — they were blessed with strong, clear voices — and came to be asked to sing at area churches, at funerals and at reunions. To this capable and willing branch of the Haynes-Wootten family passed the role of leadership for family singing practices and events.

Singers in the Woottens' community of that era often took with them to their singing sessions two or three different versions of the Sacred Harp songbook, each containing the basic core of material (including well-known songs such as "Wondrous Love," "The Promised Land" and "New Britain" or "Amazing Grace"), but each with a number of different songs as well. In the nineteenth century, there had been but one standard version of the songbook, and, when they could get it, singers used the most recent revision (1844, 1850, 1859, 1869). In the early twentieth century, the tradition splintered. The "Cooper book" revision (for its editor, W.M. Cooper of Dothan) of 1902 gained popularity in south Alabama, north Florida, south Mississippi and east Texas. In 1911, two rival revisions were published in Georgia, the "White book" (for its editor, J.L. White, son of the original author, B.F. White) and the "James book" for its chief editor, Joe S. James). These two divided the rest of the Sacred Harp territory, the White book mainly in north Georgia and parts of northeast Alabama and the James book in the rest of Georgia, most of north Alabama, south Tennessee and north Mississippi.

The Cooper and White books had a greater proportion of the later gospel-type songs than did either the standard nineteenth-century editions or the James book, and it was the Cooper and White revisions that were mainly used where the Hayneses and Woottens lived. Family members who grew up in the 1920s and 1930s remember using the two books about evenly, though they occasionally sang out of the James book as well. Jesse Wootten had a James book and took it to singings, Freeman remembers, even if there were not many

Rod Whited

Dinner on the grounds at Haynes-Wootten family reunion, Section, Alabama, summer, 1994.

others to bolster its use. A call for a particularly affecting song would have the singers replacing one book on their laps with another from just under the bench.

The best-known version of the Sacred Harp songbook in the twentieth century, the "Denson book" (a revision by members of another great Alabama family of singers and singing teachers), first published in Cullman in 1935, was not generally used by the Wootten family until the 1950s and 1960s, when the supply of White and Cooper books gradually ran dry in their area and when family members began to venture out to singing sessions in other communities that regularly used the Denson book. Today, the family mainly uses the 1991 revision of the songbook based on the earlier Denson editions, though they continue to sing favorite songs from the White and Cooper books as well.

Over the years, the Woottens have mirrored another major change in the evolution of Sacred Harp singing: the use of the alto part. No visitor to one of the Wootten singing sessions today (the best known is the annual one at Antioch Baptist Church near Ider on the second

Sunday in April) would likely come away with the impression that alto was a late addition to Sacred Harp singing and in particular to the singing in the Woottens' immediate area of the state, but that apparently was the case.

In the nineteenth century, Sacred Harp was basically three-part music. Some songs in the book included an alto part; many more did not. But, from the earliest days, Sacred Harp singing sessions featured only three parts. Women sang tenor or treble, or doubled the bass. Newer tunebooks, however, and the increasingly popular seven-shape music, such as Christian Harmony, all employed the alto. And alto was a vital part of the new gospel-music sound, which threatened to obliterate the Sacred Harp and other older shape-note singing traditions. Eventually, the Sacred Harp yielded to the new part and to the more thickly textured sound that it brought, though not everywhere at once.

With the exception of but a few songs, the 1902 Cooper revision added the alto part throughout the book, as did the later White, James and Denson revisions. But, Carl Carmer's 1934 *Stars Fell on Alabama* details a visit in the 1920s to an all-day Sacred Harp singing on

Terry Wootten leading singing at Haynes-Wootten family reunion, New Canaan Baptist Church, Section, Alabama.

Sand Mountain — with a crowd in and around the church that the author estimates at "surely more than two thousand people" — where he noticed there were but three harmonic parts seated:

"What about altos?" I whispered to Knox.

"Don't mention the word," he said. "The real Sacred Harpers think it's a newfangled and wicked affectation. They've been having a big fight with the Christian Harmony folks about it."[2]

That description — if slightly exaggerated — fits with the memories of the oldest generation of the Woottens today. Freeman recalls that two women, "the Scroggins twins," pioneered the alto part in the singing community of his youth. One of them began to teach alto to Freeman's next older brother, Carnice, when he was just a boy. Freeman remembers the young Carnice being lifted up to stand on a table and sing alto alongside one of the Scroggins twins while she led a song.

These days young boys do not have to be recruited to sing alto at Sacred Harp events, least of all at the Wootten-Haynes singing sessions, where two to three rows of women of several generations form an alto section widely known in Sacred Harp circles for the color and robustness of its sound.

The musical strain in the Haynes-Wootten family runs both deep and wide. The Louvin Brothers, Charlie and Ira (whose real name is not Louvin but Loudermilk), once regulars as a singing-strumming duo on the Grand Ole Opry, were double second cousins of the generation of Woottens now in their prime. (Charlie has performed alone since 1965, when Ira died in an automobile accident.) Grandsons of Charlie and Rhoda Haynes Wootten, the brothers grew up hearing and singing the songs of the Sacred Harp, and over the years often credited the family singing sessions and singing style with shaping their own performance sound.

Through their cousins, Jesse Wootten's branch of the family had a chance at a wider fame, too. In the 1950s they were invited to appear on the Grand Ole Opry, with the offer, Freeman remembers, of one hundred dollars each — when "a hundred dollars was like a thousand is today." But for Pappa Jesse and his children, the Opry stage seemed an inappropriate setting for their singing, and money an unworthy inducement. They declined the offer. Better for them a country church, where people were not ashamed to show their feelings, to shout and cry while singing.

> *I want to live a Christian here,*
> *I want to die a-shouting.*
> *I want to feel my Savior near,*
> *While soul and body's parting.*

The words are from "New Harmony," one of Beulah Wootten's favorite Sacred Harp songs. Genora Tyree Meadows, another Haynes cousin, remembers her aunt's special connection to that song: "Aunt Beulah lived a long and rich life, and the one thing she prayed for was to die shouting. . . . One beautiful day at an all-day church meeting . . . she began to shout during a handshake and she was taken from this world as she had hoped she would be, shouting."

What singing represented to Beulah and Jesse Wootten and their children, and what carries over to their dozens of descendants today, can be glimpsed in an excerpt from a 1990 letter to the Chicago Sacred Harp Newsletter from one of the current generations' foremost singers, Syble Wootten Adams:

> Sacred Harp is such a natural part of my being, I had never considered or questioned "why" we sang it, or "how" we sang it. My Daddy, Chester (Check) Wootten, my Granddaddy Jesse Wootten were raised in this type singing. But, it wasn't just for entertainment or pastime. It was instead a definite part of spiritual worship. Although everyone had a good time, enjoyed the fellowship one with the other, the "singing" was a form of worship service conducted with all the respect due when you have met to sing the praises of God. . . . As the singing progressed . . . some singers or maybe a listener would feel impressed to give a "testimony" and speak of their love

for Christ and what he had done for them. As this deep feeling of spiritual enjoyment increased, and . . . the songs became more and more harmoniously sung, tears would roll down some of the singers' or listeners' cheeks and it would be a time of total enjoyment usually felt by all. . . .

Singing the songs of the Sacred Harp has, for several generations now, been at the very center of life for the Woottens. It tells them best and loudest who and what they are. Music of praise, their singing is also a wellspring of family attachment, the embodiment of shared joys and shared hopes, the harmony of brothers and sisters lifting voices together that reaches out to embrace others within the community and within the broader world of Sacred Harp singers. In a sense, it reaches across time as well, to fathers and mothers before them and surely, they feel, to generations that will follow. A great gift, at once received and shared again with others, it nears the ideal: singer, song and subject fused into one.

Judge Jackson and the Colored Sacred Harp

HENRY WILLETT

O
n almost any Sunday between the months of March and October, the seasons most conducive to travel and outdoor dinners-on-the-grounds, Sacred Harp devotees join with fellow songsters at County Line Church in Slocomb or the Mount Sinai Church in Henry County, or at any one of a dozen or so churches in the southeast Alabama counties of Barbour, Coffee, Dale, Geneva, Henry, Houston and Pike, to form the square and sing fa-sol-la. Today, approximately fifteen African-American Sacred Harp singings occur annually in the Wiregrass region of southeast Alabama.

The singing style takes its name from the songbook *The Sacred Harp*, first published in Hamilton, Georgia, in 1844. There are three revisions of *The Sacred Harp* in current use. The White revision, published in 1911 by J.L. White, is now used only in a few isolated areas of north Georgia. The most recent revision, the Denson revision, first published in 1935, is, by far, the most widely used of *The Sacred Harp* revisions. It is found at most Sacred Harp singings throughout Georgia, in north Alabama, and in parts of Mississippi and Tennessee.

Both white and African-American singers in south Alabama use the Cooper revision of *The Sacred Harp*, first published in 1902. W.M. Cooper, from Dothan, Alabama, prefaced his edition with the statement: "The selections are from the old *Sacred Harp*, remodeled and revised, together with additions from the most eminent authors, including new music." The "remodeling" Cooper referred to was the transposing of a number of songs into a lower, more easily sung key. The "revising" was the standardization of the alto part in all selections, a significant change followed by later revisers of the Sacred Harp books. The "additions" were a number of gospel songs.

This inclusion of a number of more contemporary songs in Cooper's 1902 *Sacred Harp* revision was, at least partially, in response to the surge in popularity, among both whites and African-Americans in southeast Alabama, of seven-shape note music. Where the seven syllable character note system of music had been common in the South since the mid-nineteenth century, it took on new vitality beginning in the late 1880s, with a flurry of publishing activity including many more contemporary "modern" compositions.

The Cooper revision of *The Sacred Harp* continues to be the primary book for African-American (as well as white) Sacred Harp singers in southeast Alabama. However, recent years have brought increasing popularity to an interesting *Sacred Harp* variant, first published in Ozark, Alabama in 1934. *The Colored Sacred Harp* contains seventy-seven songs, all but one composed by African-American singers from southeast Alabama and northwest Florida. Southeast Alabama has enjoyed a vibrant, if rare, African-American Sacred Harp tradition for well over a century. The Henry County, Alabama Sacred Harp Singing Convention celebrated its one hundredth anniversary in 1980. Although specific documentation is lacking, African-American slaves may well have sung Sacred Harp with southeast Alabama whites as early as the 1850s, establishing segregated conventions and singings after the Civil War. No area of the United States rivals southeast Alabama in its volume of organized African-American Sacred Harp singing activity.

The *Colored Sacred Harp* lists Judge Jackson (1883-1958) as its "author and publisher." Jackson and members of the Jackson family are responsible for twenty-seven of the book's compositions. Methodist preacher H. Webster Woods, a student of Judge Jackson, composed fourteen songs. Judge Jackson had first heard Sacred Harp singing while a teenager in Montgomery County, Alabama, and was composing tunes of his own by his twenty-first birthday. In the 1920s, Jackson had several of his compositions printed on broadsheets which he gave and sold to friends and acquaintances throughout Dale County.

In the 1930s, a committee of the Dale County Colored Musical Institute and the Alabama and Florida Union State Convention offered recommendations regarding the publishing of a new four-shape songbook. These two groups represented a powerful endorsement of the venture. The Alabama and Florida Union State Convention, founded in 1922, is the highest organizational unit in the region's African-American Sacred Harp community, the convention to which all the county conventions belong. The now-defunct Dale County Colored Musical Institute played an important role in the late 1920s and 1930s. According to Japheth Jackson, son of *Colored Sacred Harp* author Judge Jackson, "the convention voted it wanted to have a school where *our* children would learn how to write music, not just read it." The Dale County Colored Musical Institute may have been created in response to the new edition of the Cooper *Sacred Harp*, published in 1927. Judge Jackson had submitted compositions to the all-white Cooper *Sacred Harp* revision committee. They were rejected. It could be that Judge Jackson had decided on the publication of a *Colored Sacred Harp* as early as 1927. Under the "Report of the Committee" in the front of *The Colored Sacred Harp* is the following:

> We, the Committee appointed by the Dale County Colored Musical Institute and the Alabama and Florida Union State Convention offer the following recommendations: First: That we will have a musical book. Second: That the name of the book will be *The Colored Sacred Harp*. Third: That four shaped notes be used. Fourth: That Bro. Jackson be the author of the book. We hope this little book may prove a great blessing and be the means of saving souls.

The committee report was signed by fifteen members, many representing families still prominent in the African-American Sacred Harp tradition.

It is difficult to know exactly what motivations or events led to the publication of *The Colored Sacred Harp*. New, original composi-

Courtesy Japheth Jackson

Judge Jackson, 1931.

tion has always been a part of the Sacred Harp tradition. The numerous twentieth century revisions of the Cooper and Denson Sacred Harp books attest to this fact. There are a number of oral accounts of African-Americans in southeast Alabama assisting whites in the composition of four-shape songs. We know that Judge Jackson had composed songs as early as 1904. H. Webster Woods and W.E. Glanton (then president of the Alabama and Florida Union State Convention) were also composing music by the 1920s.

Probably the single most important motivating factor in the 1934 publication of *The Colored Sacred Harp* was the 1927 publication of a new edition of the Cooper revision of *The Sacred Harp*. The revision committee's rejection of compositions submitted by Jackson may have motivated him to begin planning for *The Colored Sacred Harp*.

In the Depression year of 1934, Jackson, himself, was compelled to provide the primary financial backing for the publication. Bascom F. Faust, a white banker from Ozark, and an important figure in the Sacred Harp community of southeast Alabama, provided additional financing in the amount of a thousand dollars. This may explain why the only song in *The Colored Sacred Harp* written by a white composer is Faust's "eternal Truth Thy Word." With this single exception, *The Colored Sacred Harp* was clearly the product of the collaborative efforts of southeast Alabama's African-American Sacred Harp community. In all, there were twenty-six composers; but, it was Judge Jackson who had the largest hand in composition.

The Colored Sacred Harp is an important historical document, illustrating the musical life of this Sacred Harp singing community. It

"Am I a Soldier on the Cross," by Judge Jackson, from The Colored Sacred Harp.

first appeared in 1934 at the height of African-American shape-note singing activity in southeast Alabama. Judge Jackson's son Japheth remembers that one thousand copies of *The Colored Sacred Harp* were printed. "A firm in Chicago did the printing. I went with my dad in a mule-drawn wagon to pick up the books at the Ozark train station." However, for a variety of reasons, *The Colored Sacred Harp* was not readily adopted by the African-American Sacred Harp community and had nearly disappeared from the community's active repertoire before its first reprinting in 1973. One might have expected *The Colored Sacred Harp* to have been widely embraced considering the careful crafting of the composition committee to include a variety of families from a number of counties throughout southeast Alabama. It was not.

Several causes contributed to the book's not being accepted. Because its initial appearance was during the depth of the Depression, expendable cash was scarce among African-Americans in southeast Alabama. Also, the Sacred Harp community is conservative and only slowly accepts new songs into its repertoire. Finally, it is possible that jealousy and resentment of Judge Jackson's involvement in the publication caused it to be boycotted, especially by singers from outside Dale County.

It seems that the contributing composers had received a verbal promise from Jackson that they would receive some unspecified token financial payment upon the book's publication. When the book was published, however, Jackson, already deeply invested personally, decided to delay any payment until after sales of the book showed a profit. At the time, Jackson was president of Dale County Singing Convention and was running for state convention president. He was defeated, partly the result of the controversy surrounding the book.

Although not totally accepted by the African-American singing community, *The Colored Sacred Harp* was never totally rejected. The Judge Jackson honorary sing was established in 1935, the year after the publication of *The Colored Sacred Harp*. Then, as now (the Jackson sing continues to be held each year on the third Sunday in April), participants set aside periods for singing from *The Colored Sacred Harp*.

Ironically, in the 1990s, with a steadily decreasing number of active African-American Sacred Harp singers, *The Colored Sacred Harp* is enjoying its greatest popularity. It has undergone three reprintings since 1973. This new-found popularity is the result of scholars outside Alabama discovering *The Colored Sacred Harp*. As a result, the African-American singing community has rediscovered the book. Old jealousies and resentments were dying just as the older singers were dying. The singers developed a new sense of the historical significance of the songbook. As the singing tradition began to wane, attracting fewer and fewer active participants, *The Colored Sacred Harp* became a symbol of pride among members of Alabama's African-American shape-note singing community.

The Deasons: A Christian Harmony Family

ANNE H. F. KIMZEY

A t the most recent annual Deason Reunion, family members from fourteen states returned to Bibb County, Alabama, to reconnect to each other and to their heritage. For three sunny, autumn days they participated in group activities such as a family golf tournament, sack races, an egg toss, a barbeque, and the annual business meeting. But the most meaningful way that the family chose to celebrate their heritage was by gathering on a Saturday at the Little Hope Primitive Baptist Church in Eoline to sing out of the *Christian Harmony* songbook.[1]

They sang the way they, their parents and grandparents had always done—assembled in the shape of a square, according to voice part, with the song leader directing from the center. Ola Deason Meadows directed "Raymond" (#135). She and the group sang the names of the notes through first, then, in strong, clear voices, sang:

My soul, come meditate the day,
And think how near it stands,
When thou must quit this house of clay,
And fly to unknown lands.[2]

Latisha Crocker chose "Webster" (#21), by the seventeenth century composer Isaac Watts, which seemed to hold particular meaning for the group of singers in the words:

56

Sing till we feel our hearts
Ascending with our tongues,
Sing till the love of sin departs,
And grace inspires our hearts.

Sing on your heav'nly way,
Ye ransomed sinners sing,
Sing on rejoicing ev'ry day
In Christ the blessed king.[3]

Before Carver Deason led the group in "Sing His Praise" (#273), a song he composed for the 1958 edition of the *Christian Harmony*,[4] he spoke of how he had been coming to the church all of his life, and how he was there that day to honor the memory of his parents, grandparents and great-grandparents and their belief in God. When a group of Art Deason's sweet-voiced granddaughters led "Happy Land" (#289) and "Indian Convert" (#287), two of the first songs their grandfather had taught them, several of the other singers were moved to tears of joy.[5] After singing all morning, the group broke for "dinner on the

Joey Brackner

The Deason family and friends.

Christian Harmony singer Art Deason at Capitol City Shape Note singing.

grounds," a home-cooked feast served on tall, concrete tables under a long shed by the church. As the reunion issue of the family newsletter later proclaimed, "when the Deasons meet, there is good singing and great food to be enjoyed by all."[6]

The *Christian Harmony* was originally published in 1866 by South Carolinian William Walker, author of the extremely popular four-shape tunebook, the *Southern Harmony* (first published in 1835). In the *Christian Harmony*, Walker switched to a seven-shape notation (do re mi fa sol la ti) from the traditional four-shape system (fa, sol, la, mi), adding many new compositions, and expanding the harmony to four voice parts, rather than the three-part harmony of many of the tunes in the *Southern Harmony.*[7]

The use of the book spread throughout the South through the efforts of itinerant singing school masters who spent about two weeks at a time in various rural communities, teaching students to read music by a system of seven distinct shapes designating the notes of a scale.[8]

The proprietorship of the book shifted to Alabama in 1958 due to the strength of the tradition in the state and to the initiative of certain singers who determinedly promoted the music.[9] According to Christian Harmony singing master Art Deason of Centreville, the tradition had become threatened because the supply of books was so exhausted that there were "not even enough (copies) to have an all-day singing or to teach a singing school."[10] His cousin John Deason and another singer, O.A. Parris revised the 1901 edition, leaving out one hundred and eighty-eight tunes not often used, and replacing them with one hundred and nine new tunes by the members of the Deason family, by Parris, by well-known gospel hymn composers of the twentieth century, such as A. P. Bland, J. R. Baxter, Jr., W. H. Doane, A. J. Showalter, Benjamin Unseld, and John B. Vaughan, and by modern *Sacred Harp* composers A. M. Cagle, John Hocutt and S. Whitt Denson.[11]

Not until 1994 when the Christian Harmony singers were faced with another book shortage, did they decide it was time for a new revised edition. This preservation-minded revision committee (Art Deason, John T. Hocutt, Col. R. H. Yarbrough, Elder Donald Smith, Harvey Dockery, and Benny Rigdon) replaced only a few tunes this time and corrected the notation on another few to make them "more singable," said Deason.[12] They also included the Rudiments of Music[13] from the 1873 version that had been omitted in the 1958 revision.[14]

Art Deason, the acknowledged patriarch of the Christian Harmony singing community in Alabama, has devoted a lifetime to perpetuating his family's musical tradition. He was born in 1909 in Bibb County and claims, "I began singing when I was old enough to sit in my mother's lap." His family worshipped at Little Hope Primitive Baptist Church one Sunday per month and attended Christian Harmony singings on the other weekends.

The Deason Family Christian Harmony Singers at Alabama Folklife Festival.

At the age of six he attended his first of many singing schools. At age twelve, he attended a school taught by his cousin John Deason, who would become one of the *Christian Harmony* revisionists. In his teens he also studied music under faculty of the James D. Vaughan Music Company and the Stamps-Baxter Music company, publishers of seven-shape hymnals. Art Deason taught his first singing school in 1936 and has served as music director for churches of several denominations, including Baptist, Methodist, Nazarene and Presbyterian.[15]

While he has experience teaching many types of sacred music, he demonstrates a special appreciation for the shape-note tunes of his ancestors. "For the last fifteen years I have devoted my singing school teaching activities entirely to *Christian Harmony*," he explained.[16]

Deason and younger Christian Harmony leaders, such as Donald Smith and Benny Rigdon, have conducted singing schools in the Alabama counties of Bibb, Tuscaloosa, Hale, Perry, Jefferson, St. Clair, Montgomery, Cullman and Etowah, to name a few. In recent years, the financial burden of organizing schools has been offset by Folk Arts Apprenticeship grants from the State Arts Council and the National Endowment for the Arts in recognition of the importance of Christian Harmony singing to Alabama's musical heritage.[17]

Art Deason believes that the power in the message contained in these songs and the joy of performance are two reasons Christian Harmony singing still carries on today. He explained that the singing is "a form of worship" and that the songs "give a spiritual lift" to the singers.

"These tunes are different," he said. "(Some of) these tunes came to us from England, possibly two hundred years ago. And some people say they have a doleful sound, a mourning sound. But I think, back in the beginning in our country, it was the feeling that our people accepted and loved enough to instill it into our children and the other folks' children."

Deason believes that this singing has a practical purpose for young people as well. "This type of singing gives them something to do rather than to get into things that they shouldn't be doing. And I think it's steering them in the right direction," he explained. "There's a real message in some of the old songs that will guide them right."[18]

Seven-shape-note Gospel Music
in Northern Alabama:
The Case of the Athens Music Company

CHARLES WOLFE

L ate 1993 saw the death of the Grand Ole Opry's "King of Country Music," Roy Acuff. A few months later, as his executors were going through his household goods, one of them found in a closet of his house at Opryland a small box of gospel songbooks. To serious students of Acuff's musical history, this was not a surprise. During his first decade as an entertainer, as much as a third of Acuff's repertoire was drawn from gospel sources – including his famed anthem "The Great Speckled Bird." The old books he had kept came from that period; they were small, paperbacked books printed by firms like Stamps-Baxter, W.E. Winsett, and James D. Vaughan, all using a notation system that featured seven different shaped notes. During Acuff's formative years in the 1920s and 1930s, such books had dominated southern gospel music, and Acuff knew them well. Indeed, some of his own compositions had appeared in several W.E. Winsett books, years before he met Fred Rose and began the commercial success story known as Acuff-Rose Publishing.

Among the books Acuff kept over the years was one bearing the simple, but elegant title *Songs of Love*. It was published by the Athens Music Company, of Athens, Alabama, and contained one hundred and sixty pages. The price listed on the cover was thirty-five cents for a single copy, but if you could use a hundred copies, the price (postpaid) was a mere $28.50. Acuff was a young man barely out of his teens when the book came out, and back home in Maynardsville, Tennessee, he was busy learning to play the fiddle by listening to Am Stuart records. How he got the book is still a mystery. Did he acquire it at a rural singing school taught by one of the writers in the book? Did somebody he knew give it to him in later years – perhaps one of the singing Delmore Brothers, with whom he toured when he first came to the Opry? Did he find it himself, and recognize an old song he knew in its pages? And why did he choose it to keep out of all the thousands of books of music he was sent over his long career as perhaps the nation's most recognized country singer?

We probably will never know the answers to most of these questions, but the very presence of the Athens book in Acuff's collection is in itself revealing. It is one instance of many that illustrates the surprising influence of a tiny Alabama publishing company that only stayed in business for a few years. One of the dozens of grassroots gospel publishing companies across the South in the early decades of this century, The Athens Music Company had an effect far beyond its original goal and geographic setting. It became the locus for several of the most important figures in southern gospel music, and the inspiration for a number of key figures who were to take the traditional gospel sound into the mainstream of American pop and country music.

No serious, comprehensive history of southern gospel has yet been written; the music is one of the last remaining uncharted regions on the map of American cultural history. It is, therefore, hard to assess the final role of Alabama, and the Athens Music Company, in that larger context. We do have a generally accepted definition of "southern gospel;" according to the National Academy of Recorded Arts and Sciences (NARAS), the organization that gives out the annual Grammy awards, southern gospel is to be distinguished from "soul" gospel (African-American gospel), "contemporary" gospel (praise music and contemporary Christian music), and choral music. Southern gospel is primarily Anglo-American, southern in origin, often associated with small group singing ("four men and a piano" is a favorite quip), some times utilizing the instrumentation of country music, and derived from earlier folk and shaped note traditions. Its modern stars might not include Amy Grant or Take 6, but groups like The Kingsmen, The Gold City Quartet, The Cathedrals, and many of the artists featured in the various "Reunion" projects of Bill and Gloria Gaither. Its tradition has embraced everything from songs like "I'll Fly Away" to the gospel music of Elvis Presley.

One of the preliminary findings about the history of southern gospel is that, although it is properly regarded as a cousin to country music, it developed along radically different lines than did country. Country music moved directly from an oral folk tradition to a largely oral commercial tradition. It also moved quickly from its rural origins to southern urban centers like Nashville, Atlanta, Dallas, Wheeling, Cincinnati, and others. It professionalized – that is, its practitioners were able to make a living at it – within barely a decade (1925-1935). Its main commercial forces were radio broadcasting companies and their sponsors, commercial record companies, and talent/booking agencies.

Southern gospel, on the other hand, was always bound up in a written and printed music tradition. It was the music publishers like James D. Vaughan and Stamps-Baxter who began to hire quartets to travel around and sing their songs. From the period of 1910 to 1960, southern gospel was motivated not so much by radio or records, but by the small, paperbacked, shape-note songbooks, and the companies that produced them. The first gospel quartets were hired not as an end in themselves, but to popularize new songs from new songbooks, and to sell these songbooks to rural singers and churches throughout the South. Unlike the old printed or handwritten ballad lyrics the country singers sang from and then often committed to memory, the new gospel songs were sung directly from the music books, often by singers who were fully capable of reading the notes on the printed page. The center for performance remained the local church or county singing convention, not the urban media center; the gospel songwriters often remained in their own small communities, and mailed in to the publishing company their compositions for editing and eventual publication. Thus the music remained largely decentralized, with much closer ties to the community and local culture. And while some of the publishing giants like Stamps-Baxter themselves eventually located in Dallas, many smaller publishing companies remained in relatively small towns like Lawrenceburg, Tennessee (Vaughan), Hartford, Arkansas (Hartford), Hudson, North Carolina (Teachers), and Dayton, Tennessee (R.E. Winsett). In fact, so intense and widespread was such grassroots publishing in the period from 1910 to 1930 that no one has a complete list of all the southern publishers or their products; in 1933 George Pullen Jackson, in his landmark *White Spirituals in the Southern Uplands*, listed some twenty-nine such publishers, but modern researcher Harlan Daniel has estimated that the true number is probably twice that. Most publishers issued a new book once a year (some of the more successful did two), and from 1910 to 1930 each book was selling on the average some ninety thousand copies. Such numbers are impressive even by modern standards, and far exceed the sales of early commercial country Victrola records. They also indicate the extent to which gospel music impacted southern culture in those years.

The history of "convention" or "seven-shape" gospel music I have traced elsewhere; it began with the Reubusch-Kieffer Company at Dayton, Virginia in the days after the Civil War. The newer music featured songs that emphasized personal salvation rather than more philosophical songs about the nature of man. The newer songs were also more optimistic, and many of them adapted a philosophy akin to that of the best-known song of the genre, "Give the World a Smile Each Day" (1927). Originally, the newer songbooks were designed not so much for formal church services, but for special singings and for "singing conventions" in which many of the singers in a county-wide area might gather to try their hand at sight reading the songs in the new books. In some areas, competitions were held to see who could sight sing or direct songs they had never seen before; for this reason, it was important that the songbooks contain brand new songs, and they be issued on a regular (often annual) basis. As publishers began to hire quartets to go around and sing samples from the latest book, local singers and churchgoers began to like the idea of sitting back and being entertained by these skilled, semi-professional singers. During the 1930s and 1940s, the tail began to wag the dog; the quartets found that the audiences were more interested in them than in their publishers or their songbooks. Gradually, some of them began to break away from the sponsorship of the publishers, and go out on their own. The John Daniel Quartet, from Sand Mountain, was one of the first and most successful of these. Originally representing the James D. Vaughan company — one of some sixteen working for them — the Daniel Quartet made the break in the 1940s and soon found a home on Nashville radio station WSM and the Grand Old Opry. Many other singing groups soon followed suit.

North Alabama emerged as a bastion of this kind of gospel tradition; more important figures in the music came from here than from any other state except Texas. Not coincidentally, this region — defined in this study as the part of the state north of and including Birmingham — was also one of the last strongholds of the older Sacred Harp music. Several key figures in convention music, in fact, were also active in the Sacred Harp tradition, and served as key transition figures between the two musics. These included S. Whitt Denson from Cleburne County; John Dye from Shelby County; O.A. Parris, from Jefferson County; and Otis McCoy, who worked for many years with the Tennessee Music and Printing Company. The area was also home to a number of music publishers, such as The Ganus Brothers, The Denson Company, the Parris Company, and the Convention Company, in addition to the Athens Company. J.R. Baxter, Jr., one of the cofounders of what became the South's largest gospel publishing company, Stamps-Baxter, was a native of Lebanon in DeKalb County. Important composers such as W. Oliver Cooper, Vep Ellis, V.O. Fossett, John W. Vaughan, and Eugene Wright, all of whom became well-known figures in the new movement, hailed from this area. Performers who took the convention music out of the region into a much wider popularity on radio and records include groups like the aforementioned

John Daniel Quartet, the Speer Family, country gospel greats like The Delmore Brothers and the Louvin Brothers, and key quartet singers like Jake Hess and Bobby Strickland. A preliminary check-list of key figures in north Alabama's gospel music history appears in the Appendix below. Detailed research on many of them is sparse or incomplete, and not until historians better learn their stories can anything like the full story of southern gospel in Alabama really be told.

There are few people left today who have any direct, first-hand knowledge of the Athens Music Company. One of them is Jesse "Jake" Williams, a remarkable singer and songwriter who still lives in Athens. Jake's father, William Anderson (W.A.) Williams, was a key songwriter and supporter of the company, and played an important role in its founding. W.A. was born in 1874 at the south Tennessee hamlet of Tarpley's Shop, but grew up in Elkmont with his uncle, Tommy Compton. As a young man, he worked as a laborer on a steamboat on the Elk River, hauling cordwood and logs to market. Soon he met and married a local girl, Lota Hasseltine Rogers, and settled on a farm in the fork of the river. The pair eventually had ten children.

The family attended the nearby Mt. Carmel church, where W.A. got interested in singing. Sometime about 1913 or 1914, the church decided to bring in a teacher to conduct a singing school. This was a common practice in those days, and most schools consisted of class instruction on the "rudiments" of church singing; the main purpose was to improve the singing skills of the church, but in this case, the teacher also agreed to stay over and conduct a normal school for the better singers. W.A. was one of these, and soon was trying his hand at writing songs as well as singing them. By 1915 one of his efforts, "On That Bright Heavenly Shore," was good enough that it was published by a company called Firm Foundation. During the next several years, he published several songs in other books; some of them were co-authored by his sister-in-law, Sue Ellen Chitton, and others with his sons – including Jake.

The person who came down to lead the singing schools, and the person Williams feels was the initial inspiration for the formation of the Athens Music Company, was George W. Bacon. Originally from North Carolina, Bacon later moved to White Pine in East Tennessee, where the started his own organization, The Syulva Music Company. Like many late nineteenth century gospel composers, Bacon had extensive credentials and formal training, and was as much at home with classical music as with gospel. He had studied with, among others, E.T. Hildebrand, and was a specialist in harmony and composition; he composed some three hundred marches and waltzes for the piano in addition to songs like "The Judgement Morning" and "Dearer Than Ever." Jake Williams recalls: "Mr. Bacon, he could play an organ, even though he had three or four fingers cut off or missing; but, he could play an organ like anything. And they said that he knew all the music that they had in the United States, and was taking lessons from some other nation over there somewhere." It was Bacon who taught and encouraged W.A. Williams to begin writing.

By 1924, according to one source, several people in the area had decided to organize a new music company. One inspiration, certainly, was the James D. Vaughan company, fifty miles to the north at Lawrenceburg. By 1924, the Vaughan company had been in operation over twenty years, and was the most successful such company in the South; its books were selling, its normal schools at Lawrenceburg were oversubscribed, it had begun a record series featuring its several quartets, and it even sported a monthly magazine, *The Vaughan Family Visitor*. It was also putting Lawrenceburg on the map; not only did thousands come to the town to study, but the company even started its own radio station. Such lessons would not have been lost on the town fathers of Athens — especially when good singers and songwriters like W.A. Williams were mainstays of the board of County Commissioners.

Selected to manage the new company was a local singer and writer, Charles Albert (C.A.) Brock. Brock had begun his family in a two-room cabin in Cullman County, where even the children helped pick cotton to make ends meet; a few years later he moved across the line to Cedar Point, Tennessee, where other branches of the Brock family lived. There too they became members of the Methodist Church, and the Brocks' younger daughter Lena began to play the piano for services. C.A., in the meantime, was establishing a reputation as a singer, writer, and singing school teacher, and about 1910 he moved to Athens from Gadsden. "He had a quartet," Jake Williams recalls. "Him and his daughter and his son-in-law, G.T. Speer. They used to come down here to sing a lot. They'd stay at our house and put on concerts around the country." Among Brock's five children was Dwight, who was a spectacular piano player. He would, in fact, emerge as one of the great innovators of gospel piano accompaniment, recording extensively for Victor and merging jazzlike rhythms with the new up-tempo quartet songs. "As far as I know, I was the first rhythm piano player on gospel songs," he recalled. "I learned a lot of my piano from my father, and took lessons from Anita Crider. I finished high school in Athens, and learned all I knew about the piano at that time. I practiced about eight hours a day." In 1927, he joined the new Stamps Quartet and traveled with them to Atlanta to make their first recordings; one of the cuts was one of the first recordings of "Give the World a Smile Each Day," a best-seller which became a southern gospel standard – and the piano parts for which had young pianists all over the South sitting up to take notice.

The third key figure in the company – in addition to Brock and Williams – was thirty-three-year-old George Thomas (G.T.) Speer, Brock's son-in-law. In later years, he would become known as "Dad" Speer, the genial patriarch of one of southern gospel's singing dynasties, The Speer Family. But, in 1924 he was simply Tom Speer, living with his new bride in the little community of Double Springs, about eight miles from Athens. In later years, he was fond of telling interviewers that he "met a singer's daughter at a singing convention, got married in a singer's home, and raised a singing family." And, in fact, he had met Lena Brock at a singing school taught by her father, and had eloped from W.A. Williams home; the pair had married in Athens in 1920. Growing up in Cullman County, young Tom had spent a year fighting in France in World War I, before he had begun to study with George Bacon and with another local composer, T.B. Mosley. After

Courtesy of Charles Wolfe

The Speer Family, circa 1930.

their marriage, G.T. and Lena sought to supplement their income by announcing themselves as "Vocal Instructors" and "Evangelistic Singers" — both with "Reasonable Rates." They soon formed a quartet with Tom's sister Pearl and her husband William Claborn, and considered going at music full-time. Complicating all this were the births of two children, Jack Brock (in 1920) and Rosa Nell (in 1922).

All of these elements came together in 1924 when The Athens Music Company issued its first book, bearing the hardly imaginative title *New Gospel Hymns*. It was printed by the same printer used by the Vaughan Company — the Armstrong Company of Cincinnati, a venerable establishment which retained the veteran typesetters who were able to create the unusual shape notes needed for the book. Also following the model set by Vaughan, the book contained some one hundred and fifty-five songs, about 80 percent of them new — *i.e.,* appearing in print for the first time in this book — and the balance older standard hymns like "Stand Up For Jesus" that were used as half-page fillers. On the title page, some one hundred and nine songwriters are listed as contributors, but a handful of writers contributed most of the songs. C.A. Brock himself is credited (usually for the music) with some twenty songs; G.T. Speer is given credit for sixteen titles. Song No. 1 in the book is "The Glory Land," by C.A. Brock with words by Mrs. C.A. Brock. Many of the songs are on standard themes, but some have personal touches; C.A. Brock's "A Dear One Gone" is dedicated "in memory of our little Clyde," a son the Brocks lost in 1910; and G.T. Speer's "When We Cross the Rolling Tide" was written in France as he was preparing to return from World War I. (Such details are provided by dedications and headnotes to the songs.)

Given the age and time, a surprising number of women writers appear in the pages — often as wordsmiths. Katharyn Bacon, wife of George, contributed numerous lyrics, though none to music by her husband. Stella May Thompson, who wrote for Vaughan's company, also appears quite often, as do names like Adelle Justice, Laurene Highfield, Maggie Sharpton, Almira Bottoms, and others. W. Oliver Cooper, who was on the threshhold of a long and eventful career as a composer, also appears with two songs, as does Dwight Brock, the pianist. Other names appearing often include M. Elgar Belue, Berry B. Gatlin, W. Chester Dollar, and W.S. Hess.

The last-named writer, who contributed a song called "'Tis Sweet to Remember" to this collection and would later contribute to the other collections issued in Athens, was another well-known singer in Limestone County. Hess would eventually have seven children, four of whom he would mold into a children's quartet. One of these was W. Jake Hess, who would in a short time become one of the most influential lead singers in gospel music. Jake, who was born in 1927, right in the midst of the Athens Music Company's lifespan, recalls that he began working with the Hess Brothers when he was only five. "I was just a kid, but I was the star, because they had to stand me on a chair for people to see me. The saddest day of my life came when I grew up and realized that people liked me because I was young and not because I could sing."

The company also ran low-key advertisements in the book, again in the manner of other publishers. There were no other songbooks to advertise, but the mainstays of the company were always interested in getting work as singing school teachers or song leaders. "If you are in need of a Song Leader for Revival Meetings, let us hear from you, for we have them." The company also planned to hold an annual Normal School in Athens "beginning on the Second Monday in January, 1925." This was apparently not successful, for no later notice is taken of it in later books.

With the growing success of the Speer Family and the travels of Dwight Brock, the Athens books began to sell, and to carry their songs across the South. After *New Gospel Hymns* was issued in 1924, new books became an annual event. 1925 saw *Songs of Love*, the first book to carry C.A. Brock's name on the masthead as editor; 1926 brought an even more influential collection called *Bright Melodies*, and in 1928 a volume called *Praises of Jesus*. By this time, the publishers realized that the more versatile they could make their books, the more copies they could sell; they explained on the title page that the book was suitable for "The Sunday School, The Singing School, The Singing Convention, And All Kinds of Religious Work and Worship." By this time, C.A. Brock and G.T. Speer were such mainstays of the company that when George Pullen Jackson compiled his list of publishers for *White Spirituals in the Southern Uplands*, he cited the company only as "Brock and Spear" [sic] of Athens, Alabama.

In later books also began appearing another composer credit that was to have considerable impact on southern music. In *Songs of Love* in 1925 appeared a song entitled "Bound for the Shore," with credits to Mollie Delmore and Alton Delmore. This marks the first published song by the senior member of the Delmore Brothers, arguably the best folk composers to come out of Alabama, and members of the Songwriters Hall of Fame. Mollie Delmore was Alton's mother, and W.A. Williams was Alton's "Uncle Will." The following year's *Bright Melodies* found two more Delmore songs, "We'll Praise Our Lord" and "The Vision of Home, Sweet Homes." The 1928 book *Praises of Jesus* contained "What a Moment of Gladness," penned by Alton and Mrs. Bacon, and "My Blessed Guide," written by his mother in collaboration with Maggie Sharpton. According to Jake Williams, Mrs.

Courtesy of Charles Wolfe

The Delmore Brothers in the 1940s.

Delmore's contribution to the pieces was not token; "as good as Mollie was," he recalled, "she probably did the bulk of the writing." Alton in 1925 was only seventeen years old.

In his autobiography, *Truth is Stranger Than Publicity,* Alton recalls pestering his mother until she taught him how to read shape notes. He also recalled what came of it. "I did quite a bit of singing back in those days. I had written my first song....and it came out in a book about the time we moved to Decatur. All the quartets knew of this and despite the fact that I could never sing loud they all wanted me to sing with them....There was one fellow who was so persistent about keeping a quartet that he would drive miles to pick up a singer that he needed." By the time he was ready to make his mark as a country singer, Alton knew how to sight read out of a songbook, knew rhythm and timing, and knew how to harmonize. He would become one of the first country singers to get a solid grounding in the old singing convention system.

∽

The brilliant run of the Athens Music Company ended in 1929, when the songbook series suspended publication. Tom Speer was working a day job as an insurance salesman, and his company decided to transfer him up to the larger town of Lawrenceburg, Tennessee. As the Depression deepened, the insurance business failed to improve, but, as luck would have it, Lawrenceburg was the headquarters for the Vaughan music company, and within a few years Tom was working full time for them. Like most people at the start of the Depression, Tom and C.A. Brock assumed the hard times were temporary, and they hoped they could eventually continue with their Athens books. They never did. The Speer Family followed the path of so many gospel singing groups and eventually broke from the Vaughan company to strike out of their own. By 1941 they had their own radio show in Montgomery, Alabama – just before another live show by a young singer named Hank Williams – and by the 1950s they were pioneering gospel music on television. In 1956 members of the family, including young Brock, sang back-up for Elvis Presley on his first RCA Victor session in Nashville.

W.S. Hess remained in the Athens area, and watched his son Jake graduate from high school there. Soon Jake was singing with The John Daniel Quartet, another of the pioneering groups that broke its early association with Vaughan and started off on its own. By 1948 Jake had graduated to The Statesmen, one of the most dynamic and popular of all southern quartets; here he developed a lead singing style that had a substantial impact on not only gospel, but American music in general. One of his fans was a young Elvis Presley, who once played one of Jake's old Statesmen records for a friend, and said, "Now you know where I got my style."

In 1933 Jake Williams helped drive Alton and Rabon Delmore up Highway 31 to Nashville, where they began appearing on the Grand Old Opry. Within a couple of years, the brothers were the most popular act on the show, and recording extensively for Victor's Bluebird label. Though their biggest hits were new original songs like "Brown's Ferry Blues" and "Gonna Lay Down My Old Guitar," they continued to feature duet versions of many of the old convention songs they had grown up with. These included "Are You Marching with the Savior," "I Need the Prayers of Those I Love," and "Won't It Be Wonderful There." In the 1940s the Delmores would earn a place in rock and roll history as they merged blues with country in classic recordings like "Blues Stay Away From Me," an original arrangement in which Alton used the harmony techniques he had learned with the Athens company. And in 1952, at one of their final recording sessions, the brothers recorded a version of the old Athens song "Bound for the Shore."

Today little remains of the Athens Music Company except a few memories and some tattered songbooks. Few libraries have files of the books; the copies used for this research came from Jake Williams, who found them stuffed behind a fireplace in an old house. They are fragile, worn, and have names and song numbers written on their covers; above all, they have been used, sung from by generations of anonymous singers who saw the music as part of their heritage, and as nourishment for their values. In this, ultimately, lies the real importance of such gospel music; its creators were not the callow professional tunesmiths of New York's Tin Pan Alley or the sanctimonious and self-conscious composers on Nashville's Music Row, but the farmers, small businessmen, teachers, railroad workers, mothers and sons of the small towns across the South. It was a true grassroots music, for the people and by the people. Yet it was a music that did spread its influence far beyond the small towns and rural churches. And, in the case of The Athens Music Company, it represented a convergence of a rare number of talents — talents that would reach far beyond northern Alabama to literally help change the face of American music.

EARLY SOUTHERN GOSPEL FIGURES FROM NORTH ALABAMA: A PRELIMINARY CHECKLIST

BARRENTINE, CARLOS. Born 1895, Coal (Walker County). A pupil of J.D. Patton, composer of the popular "We Shall Rise;" best known as a teacher in Jasper area.

BARRY, CLARA MOORE. Born 1901, Reform (Pickens County). One of the major figures in southern gospel publishing; co-founder of Stamps-Baxter publishing company; accomplished composer; later worked out of Dallas, where he died in 1960.

BROCK, DWIGHT MOODY. Born 1907, Gadsden (Etowah County). See article for details.

BROCK, L.O. Born 1878, Georgia. Though born in Georgia, this teacher and composer spent much of his career in Cullman.

COLLIER, JOHN ALBERT, Born 1888, Horton (Marshall County). Studied at T.B. Mosley's singing school at Albertville; later taught and lived in Guntersville.

COOPER, W. OLIVER. Born 1885, Georgia, but lived in Cullman. Student of Showalter and Bacon; extensive radio work in Birmingham; editor for the Hartford Company in the 1930s; composed over 1500 songs, including the quartet standard "Looking for a City." One of the most influential convention book composers.

CLABORN, WILLIAM L. Born 1896, Winston County. In-law to the Speer Family; see above article for details.

DANIEL, JOHN. Born 1906, Boaz (Marshall County). Singer, composer, publisher; founder of the John Daniel Quartet, one of the first southern gospel groups to reach national status, over WSM's Grand Ole Opry and CBS radio. For more information, see above article.

DELMORE, ALTON AND RABON. Born 1908 and 1916, Elkmont (Limestone County). Nationally known country harmony singers who included much gospel music in their work. See above article for more details.

DENSON, S. WHITT. Born 1890, Cleburne County. One of the important links between the older Sacred Harp style and the newer seven-shape-note convention style; founder of popular Denson Trio; recorded extensively in the 1920s and 1930s; founder of Alabama State Singing Convention; publisher. In the 1930s he was joined by his son OWEL DENSON (born 1912, Arley, Winston County) in publishing revised edition of Sacred Harp.

DRUMMOND, LUTHER S. Born 1911, Jasper. Popular gospel singer in 1920s and 1930s;member of the radio group Vaughan's Happy Two.

DYE, JOHN MORROW. Born 1875, Shelby County. Composer of over 200 songs; another person comfortable working both in Sacred Harp and convention music; recorded with Riley Quartet; worked much of his life out of Birmingham.

ELLIS, VESPHEW (VEP) Born 1917, Oneonta (Blount County). Songwriter and publisher; composer of numerous songs popularized by the Blackwood Brothers in the 1950s; later worked extensively with evangelist Oral Roberts.

FOSSETT, VERNIE O. (V.O.) Born 1904, DeKalb County. Became editor-in-chief of Stamps-Baxter publishing company — eventually the nation's largest.

GANUS, WALTER POWELL. Born 1881, Wilmington (Walker County). One of two or three most important figures in Alabama gospel music, Walter Ganus founded a dynasty that included his four sons, Claude (b. 1904), Clyde (b. 1907), Clarence (b. 1910), and Cecil (b. 1912). After being a part owner of the A.J. Showalter publishing company, Walter started his own company in 1914 (eventually settling in Birmingham) and became one of the most active publishers in the 1920s. He trained many of the early commercial quartets, including the MacDonald Brothers, the first group to go out on their own as professionals. The Ganus Brothers, an act that included Walter, but featured the sons, recorded extensively in the 1920s and 1930s for major companies such as Columbia, Vocalion, and Brunswick. (One of their hit records was the later country favorite "Take An Old Cold Tater and Wait.") The family also ran a music instrument store in Birmingham for many years.

HIGGINS, WILLIAM LEE. Born 1898, Marshall County. For many years was music editor for the venerable A.J. Showalter Publishing Company in Dalton, Georgia — another North Alabama native who rose to a key position in the southern gospel publishing industry.

GIBSON, BENJAMIN M. Born 1891, Arley (Winston County). Active in Arkansas and west Tennessee, recorded for Victor as member of the Missouri Pacific Quartet.

GILLILAND, BENJAMIN FRANK. Born 1874, Shelby County. Published song books for 14 years, lived much of the time in Bessemer.

GOFF, ANDREA. Born 1939, Hueytown. Wife of Jerry Goff and member of the modern group The Singing Goffs; often seen on Birmingham and regional television.

HAMILTON, PRESTON. Though born in Mississippi, lived in Jasper much of his life, became President of Walker County Singing Convention.

HAZELWOOD, AUSTIN. Born 1878, Pell City (St. Clair County). Important early music editor for John B. Vaughan Publishing Company (not to be confused with Tennessee's James D. Vaughan company); himself was a publisher until 1919; listed by George Pullen Jackson as a major Alabama composer.

HESS, W. JAKE. Born 1927, Limestone County. Legendary lead singer for the Statesmen and organizer of the Imperials. For more information, see article above.

HOOTON, MARCUS B. Born 1892, Cullman. Composed over 300 songs, organized choirs across the South.

HUFFSTUTLER, LEONARD. Born 1887, Liberty (Blount County).

Primarily a teacher, leaving Alabama to work for the Hartford company in Arkansas and the Southwest; composer of the well-known "Deep Down in My Soul;" recorded with his quartet on Vocalion records.

JENNINGS, OLIVER. Born 1901, Logan (Cullman County).

Won fame for his family group The Jennings Trio over Nashville radio in the 1940s and 1950s; spent much of his life in the Nashville area; helped popularize "His Name is Wonderful."

LOUVIN, IRA AND CHARLES. Born 1924 and 1927, Sand Mountain. Coming from a deep-seated Sacred Harp tradition, the Louvins (family name Loudermilk) merged their gospel roots with the country "brother duet" style of the 1930s. By the 1950s, they were widely known through records and on radio and were creating their own unique style of country gospel music. In 1964 Ira, who did much of the songwriting, was killed in an accident; Charlie continues to perform on the Grand Old Opry.

PARRIS, OREN A. Born 1897, Warrior (Jefferson County). One of the most influential of twentieth-century composers, O.A. Parris was yet another comfortable both in seven-shape and four-shape music. He was a key editor for the James D. Vaughan Company; later made commercial records with the Denson-Parris Sacred Harp Singers, and helped revise the original Sacred Harp book in 1936. Had his own book publishing company in Jasper; known for song "When All These Millions Sing." Upon his death in 1966, a complete book of only his songs was issued.

RAINWATER, HOWARD DEMPSEY. Born 1919, Vernon. Life-long Alabama teacher and singer, early member of Dixie Rhythm Quartet.

SHRADER, JOHN L. Born 1893, DeKalb County. Long-time Stamps-Baxter writer, best known for his "Homesick for Heaven."

SPEER, G.T. "DAD." Born 1891, Georgia. Lived for many years at Double Springs area; pioneered in taking gospel to a wider audience; family still carries the tradition today; one of the oldest dynasties in the commercial music scene. For more information, see article above.

STAFFORD, C.C. Born 1893, Blount County. Credited with over 3,000 songs and several books on theory. Later resettled in Texas.

STEVENS, THOMAS MONROE. Born 1900, Cullman County. A student of Cooper and Speer and Showalter, he was a well-known writer who lived at Vinemont.

STRICKLAND, BOBBY. Born 1920, Albertville (Marshall County). Considered by many to be the finest quartet tenor of modern times, Strickland and his family came from the Sand Mountain area; he won fame singing first with the Harmoneers and then the Statesmen in the 1940s. Organized own group, The Crusaders, out of Birmingham; idolized by young Elvis Presley; killed in an accident in 1953.

THOMAS, BENJAMIN MOSLEY. Born 1872, Georgia. Though born in Georgia, spent many years teaching on Sand Mountain; for years directed Showalter's company from Albertville. Died in 1927.

TIDWELL, WILLIAM SHERMAN. Born 1877, Marion County. A farmer and Sunday School teacher who settled around Bear Creek, he worked editing for J.D. Paton and J. Henry Showalter companies.

VAUGHAN, JOHN W. Born 1879, Heflin. Not to be confused with Tennessee publisher James D. Vaughan, who made it a habit to include a John W. song in almost every one of his books; John W. composed one of the most popular of all southern gospel songs, "If I Could Hear My Mother Pray Again," recorded by many, including the Delmore Brothers in the mid-1930s. Also wrote Hank Williams favorite, "The Old Country Church."

WILLIAMS, JOHN DANIEL. Born 1895, Lamar County. Member of quartet Happy Hitters on WBRC Birmingham for 30 years; promoted Grand Ole Singing Convention over Birmingham radio.

WILLIAMS, W.A. Born 1874, Tarpley's Shop, TN. Grew up in Elkmont; one of the key members of Athens Music Company. For more, see article above.

WRIGHT, EUGENE. Born 1907, Jasper. A brilliant young composer for Stamps-Baxter who died very young in 1943; known for "Sunset is Coming But the Sunrise We'll See" and "Where the Shadows Roll Away."

WREN, WILLIAM. Born 1882. Franklin County. Wrote for many songbook companies, including the Tuscaloosa Music Company and Denson Music Company.

WOODARD, M.H. Born ?, worked in the Birmingham area. Promoter and organizer, president and general manager of Gospel Song Publishers Association of America. Studied under Showalter and Sam Beasley.

Shape-Note Gospel Singing
on Sand Mountain

JOYCE CAUTHEN

Sand Mountain, a plateau in northeast Alabama rich in Sacred Harp singing, old-time fiddle and banjo playing, bluegrass, and country music, also has a strong and enduring tradition of shape-note gospel singing. The Sand Mountain city of Boaz, famous to shoppers across the South for its outlet stores, is better known to gospel singers as "the Capital of Gospel Singing" because of the number of singings held in the vicinity. A devoted gospel singer can attend singings six nights a week in such communites as Attalla, Happy Home, Pleasant Hill, and Skirum, and go to a two-week-long singing school in Boaz every summer.

E.C. Littlejohn of Boaz exemplifies Sand Mountain's devoted gospel singers. Born near Geraldine in 1910, he remembers attending singings with his family. During his youth, singings were important social events of the community, where young folks courted and adults kept in touch with each other. He also remembers going to singing schools. At that time there were many fine instructors, mainly due to the influence of T.B. Mosely, who had inspired great enthusiasm for gospel singing on Sand Mountain early in the century. He taught people to read and compose music and sing harmonies using a seven-shape system, as opposed to the older Sacred Harp system, employing four shapes. Those who received diplomas from Mosely could, in turn, instruct their communities in gospel singing. Mr. Littlejohn's first singing school was at Harmony, where participants were charged a dime to pay for a well bucket for the school. There he mainly stayed outside and pitched horseshoes.

At the age of thirteen, he rode with his mother and sister in horse and buggy from Albertville to Solitude to attend a singing school conducted by J.R. Baxter, who later achieved national prominence as a prolific song writer and co-founder of the Stamps-Baxter Publishing Company. There he remembers the esteemed instructor's hand as it reached over his shoulder and took away his drawing of a boy in a fishing boat.

It was Hugh Wright who got through to him. Mr. Wright would put the shape notes on the board, point at them and have each student sing them. From him Mr. Littlejohn learned that "if you've got the key tone, *do,* you don't need an instrument for the rest of them. You know what they are by the shape." From that time on he has been a dedicated "new book" singer, who enjoys sitting down with others to "read" through a paperback song book whenever a publisher brings one out.

Though the term "new book singing" is seldom used today, it was once used to differentiate it from the much older *Sacred Harp* tradition. Mr. Littlejohn's family did not do Sacred Harp singing. "All I knew was that on the first Sunday in June at Hopewell was the Old Book Singing. I didn't know a thing about it. We just went. Papa and them went because of the crowd." E.C. Littlejohn went to court his sweetheart, Daisy Belle Cobb, whom he married in 1930. He feels that he was "born a little late for the Sacred Harp. It was playing out when this was coming in."

For a few years, Mr. Littlejohn sang in the Daniel Quartet with John and Troy Daniel and Carl Rains. Daisy Belle Littlejohn was the group's pianist. It was the practice of publishing companies to sponsor quartets to introduce their new songs and stimulate book sales. Mr. Littlejohn remembers that a company "might pay for gas or let us keep some of the money from selling song books, but we never made expenses." John Daniel, however, moved to Nashville and formed a professional quartet whose recordings and radio performances met with great success.

Besides participating in gospel singing through the years, Mr. Littlejohn has also documented it. He has recorded gospel music wherever he has been with whatever technology was current—first, a disc-recording machine, then wire, reel-to-reel, and cassette recorders, and now videocamera. He has also collected thousands of paperback song books, 78- and $33\frac{1}{3}$-rpm recordings, and other memorabilia related to gospel singing. With Dr. Bobbie Glassco, who is Dean of Instruction at Snead State Community College as well as a leading gospel singer and pianist, he wrote the history of the Alabama State Gospel Singing Convention which appears in the program for each state convention. He also was vital in the creation of the Gospel Music Museum in Boaz.

Housed in the old library building at Snead State in Boaz, the Gospel Music Museum allows visitors to browse among news articles, *Vaughan Family Visitor* magazines, paperback song books, Sacred Harp and Christian Harmony hymnals, records and radio transcriptions, a pump organ, piano, U.S. Army-issue guitar, sheet music, photos of singers and songwriters, singing school diplomas, and other items related to Sand Mountain gospel music. All of these items were donated by families with a long and deep involvement in area gospel singing. The museum is open on Monday, Tuesday, and Thursday mornings.

Also at Snead State is the North Alabama Singing Convention held in the Music Building on the first Sunday in March and September at 10 a.m. Normally attracting between one hundred and two hundred singers, the March convention is small due to torrential morning rains. However, fifty hardy souls make it to the Convention and take their seats. Their seating does not reflect the four parts they sing—soprano, tenor, bass, and alto. Immediately after prayer they begin to sing their way through the three paperback song books provided by the Convention—*Singing Praise* (Vaughan Music Publisher), *Endless Love* (Ben Speer's Stamps-Baxter Company) and *Happy Hearts* (Cumberland Valley Music Company).

Truman Glassco, a retired administrator of the Marshall County School District, presides over the convention, moving about the room, notifying various singers that they will be the next to select and lead a number. As soon as one song is finished, another leader or group of leaders comes forward and calls out the name and page number of the songbook. Unless the leader brings another pianist forward, Bobbie Glassco remains at the piano and provides a strong, decorative accompaniment to the singing.

Because the song books have been out for only a few months, the singers and pianist are truly sight reading, calling on their singing-school training to get them through the song. However, they seldom call out the names of the shapes, as do Sacred Harp and Christian Harmony singers. By the time the State Convention is held in November, the new songs will be more familiar and the singing will be stronger. But then new books will be issued and these will be put aside.

During the course of the singing, no mention of composers is made, yet the singers know that among them are three writers who have songs in the new books—Odis B. Moore of Boaz, T. L. Gilley, Jr. of Fyffe, and Wayne Guffey of Lookout Mountain, Ga. Each has had more than a hundred of their songs published over the years in gospel songbooks. In particular the songs of Wayne Guffey are very popular and the Convention is delighted by his presence and his strong voice.

The Convention ends with a prayer at 3 p.m. The singing has been almost continuous since 10 a.m. with only a lunch break and a period of announcements in which invitations are extended to singings in Birmingham, St. Clair County, Cullman, Decatur, Gadsden, etc. and to the two-week long Alabama School of Gospel Music held in June at Snead State Community College.

When asked why he has devoted so much of his life to gospel music, Mr. Littlejohn replies: "You've got to do something, and it's my way of life. I love music and this is my first music. It's just like food when you're hungry."

He recalls his brother-in-law, Troy Daniel, encouraging people to sing who didn't believe they could. He would say, "The Bible doesn't say you have to sing, it says 'Make a joyful noise.'"

Today, at the age of eighty-five, Mr. Littlejohn's hearing is impaired and he has lost of sight in one eye. Both hinder his ability to sing. "I can see that I'm over the hill, but I still like to make a joyful noise." And when large numbers of folks gather on Sand Mountain to sing from the new paperback songbooks, the noise is particularly joyful.

Of related interest—

Convention Gospel Singing in Alabama

FRED C. FUSSELL

One of the more widespread of the many different forms of traditional music in the State of Alabama is Christian congregational song. Every Sunday morning thousands of groups of Alabamians, from Scottsboro to Slocomb, gather together in churches to sing their favorite Christian hymns. Most of the time this music is performed as an integral part of regular Christian church meetings—at Sunday Schools and prayer meetings, or at the Sunday morning and evening worship services that are observed by the numerous Protestant denominations. However, a significant body of music that is in use among black and white Christians is performed and enjoyed completely outside the denominational halls of Alabama's church buildings.

This musical form, with its roots solidly based in the old-time Alabama Sacred Harp singing schools, is removed from association with any specific church or denomination. It is embodied in the Alabama State Gospel Singing Convention, a non-profit organization whose activities are centered upon a state-wide coalition of local groups known as county conventions. Created expressly for the purpose of promoting and preserving convention gospel singing, the origin of the state-wide organization lies within, or at least comes out of, the Sacred Harp tradition. However, the old-time Sacred Harp custom of singing the actual names of the musical notes—fa-so-la—has been abandoned by many of the gospel convention folks. New selections of music in standard notation, much of it written by local members, is now the order of the day.

In 1994, on November 11, 12, and 13, the 64th Alabama State Gospel Singing Convention met in formal session at the Community Center in Rainbow City, a town of 7,500 located in the Alabama foothills, a few miles south of Gadsden. More than four hundred singers, representing county conventions from all across Alabama, got together and sang congregational Christian gospel songs for nearly twelve solid hours. Among the crowd, and typical of the participants in his enthusiasm for the music, was Ernest Phillips, a leader of the Lee County Convention in Auburn and a former State Convention President.

Mr. Phillips has been an active singer of convention gospel music for many years. He is an officer of the Alabama State Gospel Singing Convention, Inc. Both he and his wife, Jane, are mainstays of the Lee County group, which meets monthly at Auburn's Frank Brown Recreation Center, about a mile from the Auburn University campus. On the second Tuesday evening of each month, beginning at 6:30 p.m. sharp, an average of twenty-five members and guests meet there and sing stirring hymns and rousing gospel songs, with piano accompaniment, for exactly two hours. The room is a small meeting hall, furnished with a piano, as many folding chairs as necessary, and several countertops on which are placed stacks of songbooks. The chairs are arranged in an open-ended square. The piano occupies the open end, placed with its back toward the congregation, so that the pianist faces them. The convention singers sit or stand on the three remaining sides, altos on the left of the piano, sopranos and tenors in the center, and baritones and basses on the right. As each singer rises and takes the position of leader, standing in front of the piano and facing the congregation, he or she requests the assistance of one of several piano accompanists who are present in the group. Then the leader announces the page number, the title of the song, and the title of the songbook which contains the selection that is to be sung. The pianist then plays an introductory chord or two, the leader calls out the number of verses that are to be sung, and the song begins.

Occasionally, two, three, or even four people will stand before the group and lead together, especially if the chosen song is difficult, or if the leader is timid or inexperienced. Following the songfest, which begins and ends with a short prayer, the group adjourns to an adjoining room to share light refreshments, to socialize, and to hear announcements about the times and locations of other singings. The

Fred C. Fussell

The Lee County Congregational Gospel Singing Convention at its regular monthly meeting held at Auburn's Frank Brown Recreation Center.

gathering ends and the crowd disperses precisely at 9:00 p.m.

Many other such local conventions occur, with equal punctuality, at dozens of sites in Alabama. Some local conventions meet regularly, normally once a month. Others meet at odd times, such as only on the four or five Saturday evenings during the year that happen to fall immediately before a fifth Sunday.

The rigid formality with which the singing conventions are conducted (a precise order is maintained and minutes are kept of the proceedings) provides an interesting contrast to the various individual voices that are heard as each song is sung. Basses, tenors, altos, and sopranos all blend together with great verve and with considerable volume. A minimum of five separate songbooks are placed into use during the course of the evening. These books, each of which contains in excess of one hundred selections, are updated annually. As a result, new and unfamiliar materials are frequently "tried out" at local convention meetings. One of the aims of the individual singer is to become, through long and frequent practice, an accomplished "sight reader," one who is able to competently sing from musical notations that are unfamiliar not only to the singer who is leading, but often to the entire group. On the rare occasion when the group effort completely falters—when the tempo is lost or when the gathered singers all stumble on a line of unfamiliar lyrics—the error is taken in good humor and someone cheerfully calls out to "Try it again, 'til we get it going right!"

Non-denominational convention singing is an Alabama tradition that is far from disappearing. Here, and throughout the deep South, this form of choral music embraces a multitude of participants. In fact, it appears to be increasing in popularity. To learn of the meeting times and locations of Alabama Gospel Singing Conventions near you, contact Vera Miller, President, Alabama State Gospel Singing Convention, Decatur, Alabama, (205) 353-6564.

Community and the Jefferson County, Alabama, Gospel Quartet Tradition

DOUG SEROFF

I n Jefferson County today, the African-American community continues to nurture its deep sacred harmony quartet traditions, just
as it has since the 1920s. Virtually all the older gospel groups
who preserve this venerable heritage include at least one member
whose quartet singing experience extends back before World War II.

At times, it seems traditional American music is inseparably linked
to a vanishing generation. The very purpose of community-based traditional music has come into question in recent decades. Popular music,
including African-American gospel music, has become a commodity
vigorously advertised and marketed in every American community
and home. A network of universities, nightclubs, publicly-funded festivals and arts programs provide venues and audiences for a small number of traditional music stars, but perhaps the ongoing *living culture*
of at least some traditional music requires an integral local performance context and an understanding community audience.

In 1925 the function of a vibrant gospel quartet culture in Jefferson County was more tangible, having to do with the development of
the coal and iron industries and the mass immigration of African-
American families, largely from Alabama's rural districts, into Jefferson County during the early part of this century. A proliferation of
community-based gospel quartets satisfied the need for self-generated
popular religious entertainment within the segregated settlements
where African-American coal and iron workers and their families lived,
and where the black church was the effective social center.

Working communities of recent rural immigrants to Jefferson

County spontaneously produced a new style of sacred harmony singing so popular that gospel singing actually became a profitable enterprise for many local quartet groups. At least nine of Jefferson County's black gospel quartets made commercial recordings between 1926 and 1935. Dozens of Jefferson County quartet singers were traveling professionally by the year 1940. More importantly, literally hundreds of young men began long quartet singing careers in their local communities.

In the years from about 1922 to 1925, just before some of the best quartets became itinerant and left the area, practically every block in the African-American neighborhoods and settlements from Dolomite to Leeds boasted at least one quartet. The adjacent northeast Bessemer communities of Westfield, Dolomite, Brighton and Woodwards comprised one particularly creative gospel singing environment. Jefferson County's greatest quartet, the Famous Blue Jay Singers, was "hatched out" of the Brighton community in 1926. It could reasonably be said that when the Blue Jay Singers organized in 1926 gospel quartet history began.

The formation of the Famous Blue Jay Singers was accomplished by raiding three of the district's top groups: Clarence Parnell came from of Woodwards Big Four, Jimmie Hollingsworth and Charlie Beal came from the Dunham Jubilee Singers, and Silas Steele from the Pilgrim Singers in Brighton. By the time anyone got around to researching the history of Jefferson County's pioneer gospel quartets, all four of these great singers were deceased.

Aulston Moulton, the last surviving member of the old Woodward's Big Four, was on his deathbed, at his home on Oakmont Street in Brighton, when I spoke with him in 1979. Moulton said his quartet disbanded after they lost their great bass singer, Clarence Parnell, to the Blue Jays.

> They took Parnell, left me out, left Jim Steele out. The Blue Jays broke up two quartets, Dunham had one... And Steele's brother [Silas]... he went with them.

Cheryl Thurber

Downtown Brighton, Alabama.

Jim Steele was singing with Moulton and Parnell in Woodward's Big Four. Steele's younger brother, thirteen year-old Silas Steele, was poised to become Jefferson County's greatest lead singer. Tenor Jimmie Hollingsworth and baritone Charlie Beal had been singing in Westfield with the Dunham Jubilee Singers, under the tutelage of one of the area's finest quartet trainers, Son Dunham. Aulston Moulton described:

> Son Dunham, Dunham Singers. Yes, Dunham was a sho' nuff quartet set-up, he could set-up a quartet... he was a trainer... he was about one of the best there was in Bessemer at that time.

It was through the inspiration and direction of community-based quartet trainers that a distinctive regional quartet style took form in Jefferson County and was ultimately spread abroad. No similar far-reaching quartet training culture existed elsewhere.

During the mid-1930s, Mr. Sollie J. Pugh was singing bass with Jim Steele in the Edwards Singers, when Son Dunham came and picked up the whole quartet and made them the Dunham Jubilee Singers:

He [Dunham] just changed our name when we went on a trip... Dunham was with us... He wanted us to take his name and so we did do that.... We went down to New Orleans. Stayed down there about six months. We had a pretty good showing down there... Dunham was just like kind of an advisor or maybe a director. 'Cause he sang lead too. He would sing most any part when it become necessary. He sang a little baritone, a little tenor, a little bass, anything. James Allen and L.V. Cox were the ones that started me out...[L.V. Cox] sang with Dunham before I knew he or Dunham. He liked Dunham in those days...

Tenor singer James Allen was a Son Dunham discovery in Westfield, one of the promising young local quartet singers Dunham "abducted." Mr. Allen provides background:

The first quartet I sung with was there in Westfield. It was just a little club that we got up, they called the Loving Brothers...I came from Mobile in 1920... I was transferred from the shipyard to the steel car shop at Westfield. And I sang with the Loving Brothers right on up until Dunham came and he drawed me out of that group... and I sang with Dunham then. We got to going about, traveling about... We been around New York and down to Mobile and different places like, with our club and we was called the Dunham Jubilee Singers.... Dunham kind of helped to set up the Blue Jays. Dunham set the Blue Jays up before he did us. And during that time he let the Blue Jays go and taken us for his club. At that time I don't know what happened. He was a man that liked to kind of pull from place to place. He's always working out a way for hisself... Now when he got a club like he wanted them he called that *his* club... Dunham just wanted a club that he could carry them about with him, he could take over.

Courtesy of Hoover Jones and Doug Seroff

*Legendary Jefferson County gospel quartet trainer Son Dunham
with the Weary Travelers Quartet, circa 1942.*

In the process of muscling his way through the field of young
quartet singers in the Westfield-Woodwards-Dolomite-Brighton district
Dunham trained numerous important singers. His proteges included
several quartet trainers, among them tenor James Allen. James Allen
may have been ambivalent about Son Dunham the man, but he was
quick to acknowledge Dunham the trainer. It was Dunham who

equipped Mr. Allen for his own quartet training career. In the early 1930s, and for many years thereafter, James Allen held employment ostensibly singing and training quartets in the interest of Republic Steel in Gadsden, Alabama:

> Lot of chords and things Dunham tried to make, but I wouldn't never put myself ahead of him. He'd lead and when he'd come back I'd have those chords and just let Dunham hear us. But I just stayed lower. I honored him as my trainer. He learnt me how, how to sing. But still, there was lots of things he didn't know. Well, you know you can start a fellow, learn a fellow something, and he'll beat you doing it! [laughs].... Oh man, I could train a quartet. If you could talk I could train you, put you to singing.... I left for Birmingham and came to Gadsden to train a quartet for the company [Republic Steel]. And it was called the Golden Stars.... I was the trainer and the tenor. I trained those boys here for the company. Course now, at that time we was the onliest club in [Gadsden] and we sung for the company and broadcast 'round, just go about and sing for the company, and had light jobs to work, piddling around work. [Golden Stars were] about the first club ever broadcast over at WJBY [in Gadsden].

Bass singer Sam Middlebrooks was from Westfield and sang with the Dunham Jubilee Singers for a short time when he was a young man. Later in life Middlebrooks was a member of the Sterling Jubilees of Bessemer. I interviewed Mr. Middlebrooks at the home of quartet veteran Tom Lacey.

Q: What can you tell me about the way Dunham trained a group..?

SAM MIDDLEBROOKS: I know he had a something looked like a fork... Sound fork. He would give 'em... after he would hit that sound he would start it off for em, and they'd go from there... Now he was about the first man ever I seen with that sound fork.

TOM LACEY: Charlie Bridges used to train different from him. Charlie Bridges use, uh, he'd sing his song as an "O." His "O" was his "round note," he'd sing it. He'd say, "If a man would use a "O" he couldn't hardly miss his pitch in a song...."

The first Jefferson County quartet to achieve national recognition was the Birmingham Jubilee Singers with Charles Bridges. In 1926 they traveled to New York and Chicago and appeared on the vaudeville stage with Ethel Waters. They made numerous recordings for Columbia Records, which influenced African-American quartets across the United States.

Tom Lacey, who sang continuously with Bessemer-area gospel quartets from 1924 until his death in 1990, was instructed in the art of quartet harmony singing by Charles Bridges and also by Dave Brown of the Bessemer Sunset Four. Mr. Lacey had a deep love of quartet harmony singing, and throughout his adult life acted as a protecting memory, preserving local quartet lore. He proudly stated:

I was trained under them fellas see, what knowed singing.... I learnt "time, harmony and articulation" and different things through trainers who used to train me.... You take a man when he's singing, he's supposed to can sing more than one voice. If I'm wrong in baritone and you can't sing baritone, show me where I'm wrong, you can't sing! If the lead's wrong I can show him where he's wrong. If the bass wrong I can give him his chord. I may can't sing bass all the way but I can sure show him his chord. You got to put it together you got to do the best idea you can get. That's what you got to do, you got to put it together.

Chicago Defender *September 1926, advertising the first release by the Birmingham Jubilee Singers.*

For the last thirty-eight years of his life Tom Lacey was the baritone voice of the Sterling Jubilee Singers, Bessemer's oldest surviving gospel quartet group. Though he was not an original member of the Sterlings, Lacey was present on the proximate day the quartet was organized.

One evening in 1929 Tom Lacey and Charles Bridges walked across Bessemer to the segregated living quarters on the U.S. Steel Pipe Shop grounds. Bridges and Lacey went to the house of Willie Ervin, known as "Crab," where three more Pipe Shop laborers, including George Bester, were rehearsing. The Pipe Shop Workers were organizing a harmony quartet and sought instruction from Charles Bridges. Tom Lacey went along to keep Bridges company and to "help Charlie out with them boys.... Man back in them days Charlie Bridges was good. He trained a many quartet back in here and around Alabama... set up many a quartet."

The following excerpts, transcribed from conversations with Tom Lacey, reveal something about Charles Bridges' artistry, training methods and technique:

> If you use "O" [or "Oh"] when you pitch, it will give you your pitch on most any song that you sing. That "Oh" will keep you from throwing it too high. You ain't gonna say "Oh" way up there. But if you say "I," "I" will throw you way up, "E" will mostly throw you way up. But if you use "O" you know that will be the right pitch for your song... That's Charlie's stuff there. That's Charlie's method. That's what I'm talking about now.

I asked Tom Lacey what happens if the Sterling Jubilees' lead singer pitches a song way too high? Can the group bring the pitch back down again during the performance of a song?

> Well, this quartet here has not got that kind of talent. In the time of Bridges and Lot Key and Dave Ausbrooks and Jimmy Ricks [Birmingham Jubilee Singers], if they were

singing and Charlie hit that song too high, Lot [tenor] catches it under the lead. Charlie knows it was something happening, if he hit it too high and this man catches it right there in soprano *under* him, then that let him know. Directly, next time he come back where this boy was, and he [Lot Key] drop into the tenor. See all them guys could switch on stage and you never would know it...

I asked Tom Lacey: "If Charlie Bridges were to come down here now, would the Sterlings be willing to listen to what he had to say, if he wanted to go to a practice session and straighten something out?" The 83 year-old Mr. Lacey answered:

Sure. Now Charlie would start right on that lead fella. He'd get the lead part straightened out and then... the first thing he's going to get that tenor straight. And he'd sing a little baritone while he's getting that tenor straight. And next he'd get on that baritone. Directly he'd get on that bass....

Tom Lacey, Charles Bridges, Sam Middlebrooks, Sollie Pugh and many other Jefferson County quartet veterans have passed away since 1980. Their spirits continue to inform Bessemer's living gospel music tradition. Their presence can be felt at special "Anniversary" programs which quartets have held in Jefferson County since the late 1930s.

On September 11, 1994 the Sterling Jubilee Singers commemorated their 65th Anniversary of musical activity with a program at the City Hall Auditorium in downtown Bessemer. A favorite spot for programs of traditional African-American gospel music for more than two decades, the Auditorium was recently renovated, receiving a new paint job, new floor, new curtains, and, most importantly,a new and vastly improved sound system.

The City Hall Auditorium is filled with cherished memories. Singers and friends routinely congregate in front of the Auditorium before and after the program to socialize and recall old times. In this atmosphere of nostalgic reunion, one can easily imagine the shades of departed quartet greats slowly making their way down 9th Avenue again, toward the Auditorium, as they did so many times in life.

As is the custom at "Anniversary" programs, the Sterling Jubilees were praised by many speakers for their remarkable longevity, and roundly encouraged to "sing on." Among the speakers was Mayor Quitman Mitchell, Bessemer's first black mayor, who presented the honorees with the Key to the City.

The Sterling Jubilees' Anniversary program was attended by a familiar core-audience of several hundred singers and supporters of traditional gospel music, who helped make the promotion financially successful. Bessemer's gospel music public is not so large as it once was, but is extremely faithful. No doubt it's an essential part of the equation under which the a cappella harmony tradition continues to flourish. The Bessemer gospel music community treats the programs as a medium for showing respect for its musically creative senior citizens and its local heritage.

The Sterling Jubilees' 65th Anniversary provided an excellent local program of traditional gospel singing such as cannot be matched elsewhere. One characteristic feature was the presence of five different unaccompanied male quartets, with outstanding musical contributions coming from the Four Eagles Gospel Singers, the Delta-Aires and Shelby County Big Four. Additionally, the audience heard a cappella soloists, a female trio without accompaniment in a distinctively local style, and superb congregational hymn singing, including "Dr. Watts" hymns led by Ms. Luella Hatcher of Dallas County, Alabama.

The primary function of community gospel quartet programs in Bessemer and Birmingham is reverential music service. The words most commonly spoken as each new group stands to sing are "First, giving honor to God..." The progress of the civil rights movement introduced another invocation repeated at almost all gospel programs in Jefferson County, Alabama: "He brought us from a mighty long way."

A sense of the continuity of a living tradition is especially strong when octogenarian quartet masters, such as presently sing with the Sterling Jubilees and Shelby County Big Four, display their venerable harmonic artistry. During the "pinning ceremony" which marks the Anniversary, the individual members of the Sterlings and their spouses were recognized, and "pinned" with carnations and corsages. Summary histories and eulogies were given, invoking the names of Tom Lacey, George Bester, and many more former members of the Sterling Jubilees, along with the names of Charles Bridges and other legends of the Jefferson County quartet heritage, testimony to the history and continuity of this durable tradition.

Cry Holy Unto the Lord: Tradition and Diversity in Bluegrass Gospel Music

JACK BERNHARDT

Of the sacred traditions common to Alabama, bluegrass gospel music is among the most recent. Developed by Kentucky native Bill Monroe between 1939 and 1945, bluegrass gospel is the sacred counterpart to the more general secular style known as *bluegrass music*, named for Monroe's band, the Blue Grass Boys.

While it is a younger form of musical praise than, for example, Sacred Harp or jubilee, bluegrass gospel shares with them a legacy of song and worship extending from camp meetings and brush arbors, to the modern church house. And just as modern church services find their origins in earlier forms of worship, bluegrass gospel music traces its roots to secular and sacred styles derived from earlier black and white musical traditions.

Alabama has participated in and contributed to bluegrass gospel music since the genre's early years. From the songwriting genius of the Louvin Brothers and the backwoods ministry of the Sullivan Family [see Erin Kellen's essay on Margie Sullivan, in this volume], to the more contemporary sounds of Jerry and Tammy Sullivan and Claire Lynch, Alabamians have added their own creative voices, establishing bluegrass gospel music as a dynamic art form while holding to the principles established by Monroe a half-century ago.

Born September 13, 1911, near Rosine in western Kentucky, Bill Monroe was the youngest child in a family of six. His mother and siblings played musical instruments, and Bill took up the mandolin and guitar at the age of eight or nine. Monroe learned much of his music in his home and from his mother's brother, Pendleton "Uncle

Pen" Vandiver. From Arnold Schultz, a black fiddler whom Bill accompanied on guitar at community dances, he absorbed the country blues that became a cornerstone of bluegrass. And he attended the singing schools held in the Baptist and Methodist churches of Rosine, where he learned to sing harmony on the sacred songs of shape-note hymnals.

In 1934, Bill and his brother Charlie teamed professionally as the Monroe Brothers. Until their break-up in 1938, the Monroe Brothers were among the most popular of the "brother duet" acts, touring and playing daily radio shows throughout the South, and recording 62 sides for Victor's Bluebird label. Following his break with Charlie, Bill assembled a band he named the Blue Grass Boys, after his native state. At the time, his music was an extension of the string band and ballad tradition of the rural South. But determined to find a sound that was both artistically and commercially satisfying, Monroe experimented with his music and lineup until 1945 when guitarist-vocalist Lester Flatt and banjo player Earl Scruggs joined fiddler Chubby Wise and bassist Howard Watts, and the final pieces of the bluegrass puzzle were set in place.

Monroe built bluegrass upon a foundation of southern balladry and string band music, and added elements of the blues and jazz, along with Anglo- and African-American gospel styles. His visionary blend of conservative pre-war musical components with innovative lyrics and driving rhythms celebrated tradition even as it nourished the progressive yearnings of music fans in the post-war South. "I put the sound that I wanted to hear into the music," Monroe explained to me in 1988. "I had the blues, you know, I knew how to do it. And some Scotch (sic) bagpipes—that sound, the fiddle from Scotland. I put the drive in it and put the music the way I thought it should be put—the high lonesome sound. And it's got a lot of gospel singing in it."[1]

Monroe brought to his music a repertory of secular and sacred songs he had accumulated since childhood, and eclectic musical tastes that included white and black elements of style. He borrowed from the blues and other black musics, and he performed and recorded popular African-American spirituals such as "Swing Low Sweet Chariot," "When the Saints Go Marching In," and "Walking in Jerusalem Just Like John." The importance of gospel music to Monroe, and to his audience, is evident in the fact that half (thirty-one of sixty-two) of the sides the Monroe Brothers recorded for Bluebird were gospel songs, and that Monroe composed no less than nineteen of the twenty-two sacred songs the Blue Grass Boys recorded between 1946 and 1952. Folklorist Howard Wright Marshall found five themes recurrent in bluegrass gospel repertoires: individual salvation, life's rocky road, the maternal hearth, grief for the deceased, and the good Christian's "action orientation."[2] These themes are common to evangelical Protestantism, and they are the issues that concerned Monroe when he composed "Wicked Path of Sin," "The Old Cross Road," "Get Down on Your Knees and Pray," and other inspirational songs for the Blue Grass Boys' repertoire.

While singing schools, such as the ones Monroe attended in Rosine, provided an opportunity for whites to learn from whites in the Jim Crow South, there was also a continuous, fertile exchange of sacred and secular musical ideas, styles, and repertory between black and white Southerners dating from the early years of slavery. If it was blacks "who made Southern religion different,"[3] it was blacks and whites acting together who defined the essence of Southern music. The union of European fiddle music and the banjo of African origin is well known. For sacred music, blacks and whites had sung together at camp meetings, and together they defined the musical framework of the "holiness crusade," an interracial revitalization movement originating in the late nineteenth and early twentieth centuries that incorporated elements of vernacular religion, such as shouting, with modern musical instruments and styles.

Just as he had absorbed the white gospel tradition from the singing schools, Monroe was also influenced by styles of music and worship he had witnessed at the churches of Rosine. "The first singing that I ever tried to do, we'd go to church there in Rosine, Kentucky, at the Methodist, or Baptist, or then there was a Holiness church moved in later on. They sang some fine songs there at Rosine, Kentucky.

That played a part in the kind of a sound and kind of feeling that I wanted to put in my music. Taken right from the gospel sound."[4] The spirit-filled emotion that rang through the evangelical churches became an integral feature of the Blue Grass Boys' style:

> Some people, you know, don't believe in shouting in church or anything like that. Well, I have always loved to hear people shout, if they could shout. Anybody that can . . . and it does them good; I think that they should and I think that they're doing wrong by holding back; that they shouldn't be ashamed of it, and that's the same way about singing a hymn; if you feel like it and you can sing it, I believe in singing it. The colored people get to singing right from the heart, you know, and they get to living that song and that's the way that I do most of my songs . . . You know, there's holiness singing in my music, blue-grass music.[5]

Monroe found another source of inspiration in the male gospel quartets of the 1920s and '30s. White quartets, employed by gospel music publishers such as the J.D. Vaughan Publishing Co. and Stamps-Baxter Music Co., toured and conducted singing schools throughout the South, promoting the songs and songbooks of their employers and providing new sources of repertory for gospel singers. But it was the black quartets centered in Birmingham and elsewhere in the South, with their snappy syncopations, inventive harmonies, and lively performance styles, that energized quartet singing among white as well as black artists.

As early as 1927, audiences had listened to the Golden Echoes, a black quartet that performed regularly over Nashville's WSM, home of the Grand Ole Opry. In the '30s, Norfolk, Virginia's popular Golden Gate Quartet did extended stints at two of the South's most powerful radio stations—WBT in Charlotte, North Carolina, and Columbia, South Carolina's WIS, stations at which the Monroe Brothers also performed. The Monroes and the Gates both recorded for the Bluebird label, and the Gates made their first recordings in 1937 while performing on WBT.

The extent to which Monroe might have been directly influenced by these or other black quartets is unclear. But when he devised the Blue Grass Quartet, a segment of his act devoted to gospel music, Monroe applied African-American quartet techniques, such as bass lead singing, which was featured on the Monroe Brothers' recordings of "He Will Set Your Fields On Fire" and "A Beautiful Life," and on the early (1940) Blue Grass Boys' recording, "Crying Holy Unto My Lord."

A member of the Grand Ole Opry, Bill Monroe popularized his music on the Opry's Saturday night broadcasts over WSM. By the late '40s, musicians in Alabama and elsewhere were emulating Monroe's style and learning his repertoire, and bluegrass music was transformed from one artist's notion to a new genre of music.

Charlie and Ira Louvin tuned in to the Blue Grass Boys' broadcasts from their home near Henagar on Sand Mountain. The Louvin Brothers began playing professionally in 1941 and joined the Opry in 1955. They played in a style that was transitional between the brother duet acts of the '30s and a more contemporary country sound. While the close, haunting harmony that defined their music was reminiscent of the brother duet acts, they were grounded in shape-note principles that they had learned in the singing schools they attended as children. Although they were not a bluegrass act, the Louvins were among the most successful songwriting teams of their era. Several of their compositions – "Weapon of Prayer" and "The Gospel Way," – were easily refigured and incorporated into bluegrass repertoires, and their influence has extended beyond Alabama to the bluegrass community worldwide.

While the Louvin Brothers were starring on the Opry, the Sullivan Family was establishing a reputation that would earn them the unofficial title of "First Family of Bluegrass Gospel Music." For more than 40 years, the Sullivans have remained dedicated to their musical ministry, sharing their message of good news in small churches and at festivals, and on radio and television broadcasts in the vicinity of their

St. Stephens home in Washington County. If the passion of holiness theology inspired Monroe, it is the bedrock of Sullivan Family music, issuing from their commitment to the Pentecostal creed; their music is a jubilant expression of their faith, anchored more in joy than brimstone, and emphasizing salvation over the threat of damnation.

In addition to an encyclopedic repertoire of bluegrass gospel standards they learned from Monroe, the Louvin Brothers, and others, the Sullivans also feature original songs that draw from personal experiences and serve as both testimony and chronicle of their commitment to their faith. One of their most requested numbers, "Sing Daddy a Song," is dedicated to Enoch's father, Arthur Sullivan, a popular minister and the family's spiritual leader, who died in 1957 while preaching a sermon at church. "Brush Arbor by the Side of the Road" recalls the family's earliest religious experiences at a brush arbor built by Brother Arthur in the 1940s.

Over the years, the Sullivan Family band has featured a roster of outstanding musicians such as Enoch's brother, Emmett, Joe Stuart, Carl Jackson, James Phillips, and Joy Deville, but the focus has always been upon Enoch's blues-tinged fiddling and resonant baritone and the irrepressible fervor of Margie's singing. The Sullivans represent the traditional side of bluegrass gospel music as they helped define it in the 1950s and '60s. But, by adding their personal conviction and artistic vision, the Sullivan Family has advanced bluegrass gospel music beyond the scope imagined by Monroe a half century ago.

A more contemporary and eclectic sound is heard in the music of Jerry and Tammy Sullivan, who live in neighboring Wagarville. Jerry, Enoch's uncle, played bass and guitar with the Sullivan Family periodically until a near-fatal automobile accident forced his retirement from the band in 1977. Two years later he and his daughter, Tammy, began their own career, continuing the festival and backwoods ministry Jerry had worked with his nephew. Not surprisingly, Jerry and Tammy's music shares affinities with the Sullivan Family sound. For example, the two bands share elements of repertoire, and, as a youngster, Tammy patterned her vocal style after Margie's, an influence that can be heard in some of Tammy's singing today.

Jerry Sullivan

But there are significant differences between the two groups that result in vastly divergent interpretations. Jerry and Tammy draw from a wider range of white and African-American secular and sacred musics, and their repertoire extends beyond the traditional margins of bluegrass to feature other traditions. Jerry's early influences include the drop-thumb banjo playing of his father, J.B. Sullivan, who had learned banjo techniques from Alec Eason, a black resident of Clarke County. Jerry was also influenced by rhythm and blues great Joe Turner and Chicago bluesman Jerry Reed, and he has played professionally in rhythm and blues and rockabilly bands, as well as in bluegrass bands with Bill Monroe and others. A prolific songwriter who also writes from personal experience, Jerry's eclectic tastes can be sampled in such original compositions as his Cajun-flavored "The Jesus Story" and the rockabilly-styled ballad, "The Old Man's Prayer," as well as in straightforward bluegrass songs such as "Brand New Church," which he co-authored with his long-time friend, Marty Stuart.

Where Margie was inspired by the old-time singing of the Carter Family and Molly O'Day, Tammy's influences include African-American gospel greats Mahalia Jackson and Dorothy Love Coats, as well as contemporary country vocalists such as Connie Smith. Her powerful, textured mezzo-soprano, heard on songs such as "I Can See God's Moving Hand" and the *a cappella* spirituals, "Up Above My Head/ Blind Bartemus," seems to embody the Pentecostal fire that ignites the family's spiritual quest. As Tammy explains, her music is an expression of the strength of her faith:

> What I love in a female singer is power. I don't like as much a laid-back, softer voice. I like the powerful voice that gets the message out. The type of church I've been in all my life is Pentecostal. And the message, when the preacher preaches, is a driving, shouting delivery—fiery. When I go to sing, I think of that and say, well, I like that delivery that I hear from the pulpit. If I can deliver my song like that, that's the way I want it delivered and projected to the audience—with *fire* in it.[6]

Today, their band includes Tammy's younger sister, Stephanie Sullivan, on piano, and John Paul Cormier, a talented multi-instru-

Stephanie Sullivan, John Paul Cromier, Tammy Sullivan and Jerry Sullivan.

mentalist from Nova Scotia, Canada, whose Old- and New World Celtic influences dovetail nicely with and expand the catholic interests that characterize the music of Jerry and Tammy Sullivan.

Originally from Tuscaloosa, the Maharrey Family moved to St. Stephens in 1977, when Paul Maharrey replaced Jerry Sullivan as bassist in the Sullivan Family band. Over the years, the Maharreys have shifted emphasis away from bluegrass, and in 1993 they hit high on the gospel chart with "Jesus Will Heal Your Achy Breaky Heart," a Southern gospel-flavored song inspired by the Billy Ray Cyrus country sensation, "Achy Breaky Heart."

While Washington County, with its celebrated triumvirate, might be called "The Vatican" of Alabama bluegrass gospel music, bluegrass gospel also finds expression elsewhere in the state, such as in Hazel Green, where Claire Lynch has been singing bluegrass music for almost 20 years as lead vocalist for the Front Porch String Band. In

1993 she released "Friends for a Lifetime," a critically acclaimed solo album of bluegrass gospel songs that included her own composition, "Somewhere Above." Lynch's musical tastes lean toward the softer, progressive tones of the urban folk revival, giving her music a quality quite different from the rustic strains of the Washington County bands.

The Louvin Brothers' influence can still be heard at outdoor festivals and living room jam sessions in the rural communities on Sand Mountain. As its name suggests, the bluegrass gospel band, "Tradition," plays original and standard sacred songs in the style of the early bluegrass bands at churches and gospel gatherings. Morris Hicks, formerly with the bluegrass band High Caliber, is regarded as one of the region's finest gospel songwriters. His "Who Do You Know," an up-tempo bluegrass swinger, was featured on Lynch's "Friends" album.

Also in the traditional vein, the Warrior River Boys, from Cullman, include gospel songs on their albums and on stage. "Throne of Grace," a fine example of bluegrass quartet singing written by band member Mitch Scott, can be heard on their 1990 album, "New Beginnings."

As conceived and defined by Bill Monroe, bluegrass gospel music is an ebullient expression of faith that draws from a legacy of sacred and secular music from both Anglo- and African-American traditions, and transcends doctrinal boundaries. While it originated in the American South, bluegrass now enjoys worldwide popularity, and it is testimony to the transcendence of the music and the power of faith that bluegrass bands from Kentucky to Czechoslovakia routinely include gospel songs in their repertories and on recordings.

Bluegrass gospel music has sounded a chord in Alabama's faithful from the beginning, and musicians from the Louvin Brothers and the Sullivans to Claire Lynch have contributed their personal statements, making bluegrass gospel a living tradition. The diversity and vitality that characterize the state's bluegrass gospel community today will ensure the music's continued relevance and appeal well into the next century.

Of related interest—

Margie Sullivan: Mother of Bluegrass Gospel

ERIN KELLEN

Twelve-year-old Margie Brewster worked hard in the cotton fields that her family sharecropped. After her daddy sold his portion of the season's crop, he used the money he got for the cottonseeds to buy her a guitar and taught her to play. Her father's death later that year grieved Margie so deeply that her mother gave her permission to leave home to go on the road with a lady evangelist named Hazel Chain. So she left Winnsboro, Louisiana, and began traveling the Pentecostal revival circuit that stretched from east Texas through Louisiana and Mississippi to Alabama. The pair traveled by Greyhound bus and scheduled their engagements by mail.

It was dark and deserted at the crossroads where the Greyhound left them in Sunflower, Alabama, where they were supposed to conduct a revival. The loss of their luggage had delayed them for hours at the bus station in Mobile. Soon, a little boy came riding up on a bicycle and said, "You must be Sister Margie and Sister Chain." They said, "Yes." And he said, "Well, follow me," and guided them to the little church. Margie was tired, but she sang because, she says, "Wild horses couldn't keep me from singing back in those days!" That was the night she met a young man named Enoch, who played the fiddle and sang gospel music with his father, the Reverend Arthur Sullivan.

Three years later, in 1949, Margie and Enoch were married. That same month, the family's string band had its first radio performance on WRJW out of Picayune, Mississippi. They hadn't thought about what to call themselves, so they just told the radio announcer to say they were "The Sullivan Family."

For forty-five years Enoch and Margie Sullivan have been the core of the Sullivan Family—especially since banjo player Emmett,

The Sullivan Family Bluegrass Band. Margie Sullivan in center.

Enoch's brother, passed away in Spring of 1993. They called their music "Bluegrass Gospel," and they have journeyed far and wide to play it, at country and urban churches, at civic events and political rallies, at prisons, and at festivals across the United States and in Europe. In 1993, they were inducted into Bill Monroe's Bluegrass Hall of Fame at his Bean Blossom Festival in Bean Blossom, Indiana. These days they travel in their own bus, emblazoned with the words

"The Legendary Sullivan Family" on its sides.

On the homefront, in St. Stephens, Alabama, there were five children to raise. From the beginning, the Sullivans kept a small farm, raising and putting by much of their own food. Now that the kids are all grown and gone, Enoch still likes to keep a few cows and Margie still cans and freezes produce from the garden. They like to stay grounded in the unpretentious rural dailiness of their lives in little St. Stephens, the oldest town in the oldest county in Alabama. Enoch and Margie have enough working years behind them that you'd think they might consider settling down into a comfortable retirement. Instead, they keep up a pace that would wear out most people half their age.

In the early days, there were few women traveling the back roads playing bluegrass music, and most of them stayed in the background. But Margie has stayed right up front with Enoch—accompanying him on guitar, singing lead and harmony in her husky alto, writing songs, and preaching the gospel. It was through gospel music that many women entered the field of bluegrass music, most frequently through family bands like the Sullivans. Margie's prominent place in the band may reflect the family's Pentecostal background; it is not out of the ordinary for women to preach or assume leadership positions in Pentecostal churches. And the Sullivans see themselves first and foremost as spreaders of the gospel—their role as bluegrass pioneers comes second.

In fact, an examination of "string band gospel" groups like the Sullivan Family, and gospel music in general, is crucial to any investigation of the origins of bluegrass. Before anyone even called their music "bluegrass gospel," the Sullivans' performances incorporated the harmony singing, banjo syncopation, instrumental breaks between singing, and faster tempos that define the music as a separate genre. Though the southern Appalachians are stereotypically associated with bluegrass music, the phenomenon of the Sullivan Family, and other groups from the Coastal Plain, reminds us to recognize the significance of other regions' contributions to the style.

Now that women performers are so commonplace in bluegrass, it is time to take a closer look at the experiences of one of the pioneers. In the course of four decades, Margie Sullivan has transported the music from backwoods brush arbors to urban areas. She has felt the loneliness of being the sole woman traveling with men who "only wanted to talk about coon hunting and such," in the days when most male musicians had some familiarity with that pursuit. Today's women of bluegrass, like their male counterparts, are increasingly urban, middle-class, and non-Southern. Their sensibilities are shaped by circumstances radically different from those that shaped Margie Sullivan's.

Margie herself never fails to marvel at the path her life has taken. She likes to tell about the time the Sullivan Family performed seven songs at a Sunday morning service in a Catholic Church in Belgium when they traveled to Europe in 1984. An interpreter introduced each song, explaining the meaning to those who could not understand English. When they finished playing, people in the audience presented fresh flowers to Margie, as was customary. Then she, in turn, presented fresh flowers to the priest.

> "When I handed him the flowers, he reached over and kissed me on the cheek. And then he kissed me on the other cheek—that's a blessing of acceptance. And when he did that, the crowd was amazed. "So they wanted me to say something. And I was not prepared to say anything. And for just a minute I was shocked beyond words. And then I thought, well, I'll just tell them what I really feel in my heart. And I thanked them for so graciously receiving us. And I said I hope that we have represented the Sullivan Family well here today, performed in a way that was a credit to our group and our name. And I really do hope and trust that we really represented our country, the United States, real well. But more than all of that, I hope that we have really represented the Lord Jesus Christ. And I don't know why I said that. It was spontaneous. And when I said it, they stood. They went to clapping. Some of them were crying; some of them were laugh-

ing. I never saw such an acceptance. I just stood there and cried. In a big Catholic Church as long as from here to that road almost. "Oh, honey, it's beyond my fondest dreams to think that I would ever get to do anything like that. I mean, when I was singing in that cotton field, pulling that sack up and down those rows and singing with all of my heart praise to the Lord, not knowing if anybody else even heard me or not, I wasn't doing it for anybody else. But I never, you could have never made me believe I'd have the chance to do the things that I've had the chance to do."

Notes on the Essays

The African-American Covenanters of Selma, Alabama

[1] This was the opening Psalm sung at the Sunday morning worship service of Selma's Reformed Presbyterian Church on January 22, 1995.

[2] Quoted from "Who We Are: A Brief Introduction to the Reformed Presbyterian Church of North America," a pamphlet published by the Church.

[3] Lippincott, Peter, producer. *Psalm Singing of the Covenanters*, LP record and booklet. Prairie Schooner Records.

There are numerous recordings of Covenanter Psalm singing as well as various publications on the history of the Reformed Presbyterian Church. For a complete catalog write to Crown and Covenant Publications, 7408 Penn Avenue, Pittsburg, PA 15208-2531, phone (412) 142-0436, FAX (412) 731-8861.

The Moan and Prayer Event in African-American Worship

[1] Collins, Willie R. *Moaning and Prayer: A Musical and Contextual Analysis of Chants to Accompany Prayer in Two Afro-American Baptist Churches in Southeast Alabama*. Ph.D. Dissertation, University of California, Los Angeles, 1988 and Collins, Willie R. "An Ethnography of the Moan-and-Prayer Event in Two African American Baptist Churches in Southeast Alabama" in *African Musicology, vol. II*. Atlanta: Crossroads Press, 1991.

[2] In folk tradition, the humming of a Christian had been thought to be unintelligible to the devil. Humming thus was regarded as a kind of code or speech substitute. This was common knowledge over most of the South. A common saying was "When you moan the devil don't know what you're doing," although many of the informants who were interviewed questioned the truth of this saying.

[3] Newbell Niles Puckett, *Folk Beliefs of the Southern Negro*. (New York: Negro Universities Press, 1968 (originally published Chapel Hill: University of North Carolina Press, 1926). Reference is also made to a "moanin" song in George Robinson Ricks, *Some Aspects of the Religious Music of the United States Negro...* (New York: Arno Press, 1977) p. 47.

[4] Groaning also has traditionally referred to a Christian's unutterable intense yearning to be relieved from a burden. This is referred to as "groaning of the spirit." For example, when Mary confronted Jesus at Bethany regarding the raising of her brother Lazarus, the scripture recounts: "When Jesus, therefore, saw her weeping, and the News also weeping who came with her, he groaned in the spirit, and was troubled." (John 11:33).

[5] Interview, Reverend Samuel Coleman, Jr., Cotton Valley, Alabama.

[6] This definition is formulated from field data taken from the two principal churches for this study: Elizabeth Baptist church in Fort Davis, Alabama; and Spring Hill Baptist church in the Cotton Valley Community of Tuskegee in South Macon County; and from moaners from neighboring churches in South Macon County.

[7] Elizabeth Hughes Yamaguchi, "Macon County, Alabama: Its Land and Its People from Pre-History to 1870," MA Thesis. Auburn University, 1981, p. 83.

[8] Charles Octavius Boothe, *The Cyclopedia of the Colored Baptists of Alabama, Their Leaders and Their Work* (Birmingham: Alabama Publishing Company, 1895), p. 98.

[9] Reverend Anson West, *A History of Methodism in Alabama.* (Nashville: Publishing House Methodist Episcopal Church, 1893), p. 607.

[10] Interview, Deacon Theodore Samuel, Davisville, Alabama, March 6, 1986.

[11] A total of eight moans were struck during the moan and prayer event as follows: "Oh, Lord, have mercy," "Down in the valley on bending knees," "I'm gonna run on until I get my crown," "Have mercy," "Uphill journey but I'm on my way," "Said I'd serve him if he changed my name," "So glad I been born again," and "Lord, have mercy."

[12] Interview, Sister Ella Horton.

[13] As sung by Deaconess Annie Sullen, Spring Hill Baptist Church, February 6, 1986. Also see: "When You Feel Like Moaning" in Harold Courlander, *Negro Songs From Alabama* (New York: Wenner-Gren Foundation for Anthropological Research, 1960), p. 13-14. There are other spirituals which also incorporate moaning and groaning in the song text. For example, the late Reverend Malone of Spring Hill, after a sermon would lead: "You ought to moan, You ought to groan till the Holy Ghost come."

[14] Interview, Deacon Tim Menefee, *Ibid.*

[15] Interview with Reverend John Curry, Sr.

Singing "Dr. Watts"

[1] Don Cusic, *The Sound of Light: A History of Gospel Music* (Bowling Green State University Popular Press, 1990), 26.

[2] C.M. or "common meter" contains 8 syllables in the first and third lines and 6 syllables in the second and fourth; L.M. or "long meter," contains 8 syllables in every line, and S.M. or "short meter," contains 6 syllables in lines one, two, and four with 8 syllables in the third line.

[3] Cusic, 27.

[4] Rev. Samuel Davies quoted in *Readings in Black American Music*, Eileen Southern, ed. (New York: Norton, 1971), pp. 27-29.

[5] Wendel Phillips Whalum, "Black Hymnody," *Review and Expositor* (Summer 1973), 347-348.

[6] Brett Sutton, *Primitive Baptist Hymns of the Blue Ridge* (Chapel Hill: University of North Carolina Press, 1982), liner notes to recording, 15.

[7] Belle Kearney, *A Slaveholder's Daughter* (St. Louis Christian Advocate, 1900), 57.

[8] Interview with Elder Vassie Knott, Boligee, AL, November 23, 1994.

[9] Interview with the Poole Brothers, Tuscaloosa, January 23, 1991.

[10] Interview with Walter Lee, Birmingham, November 11, 1994.

[11] None of my informants have used the term "line out," a term more commonly used in white churches.

[12] Andrew Poole, January 23, 1991.

[13] Benjamin Lloyd, ed., *The Primitive Hymns* (Rocky Mount, North Carolina: The Primitive Hymns Corporation, 1989).

[14] Oliver C. Weaver, "Benjamin Lloyd. A Pioneer Primitive Baptist in Alabama," *Alabama Review* (April 1968), 144-155.

[15] Interview with Luella Hatcher, Orrville, December 11, 1989, and phone conversation, December 12, 1994.

[16] Interview with Elder Vassie Knott, Boligee, AL, November 23, 1994.

[17] Andrew Poole, January 23, 1991.

[18] Linda Reese at interview with Luella Hatcher, Orrville, December 11, 1989.

[19] Interview with Walter Lee, Birmingham, November 11, 1994.

[20] Whalum, p. 341.

[21] Whalum, 334.

Judge Jackson and the *Colored Sacred Harp*

Much of this article is taken from contributions made by Henry Willett to Jerilyn McGregory's *Wiregrass Country* (Oxford: University Press of Mississippi, 1995).

For a definitive history of *The Sacred Harp*, see Buell Cobb, *The Sacred Harp: A Tradition and its Music* (Athens: University of Georgia Press, 1978, 1989). Joe Dan Boyd has written an excellent biography of Judge Jackson, author of *The Colored Sacred Harp*, "Judge Jackson: Black Giant of White Spirituals," Journal of American Folklore, 83 (October-December, 1970), 446-451. Southeast Alabama's African-American Sacred Harp singing community is the subject of an extensive musicological analysis in Doris Dyen's "The Role of Shape-Note Singing in the Musical Culture of Black Communities in Southeast Alabama," Ph.D.dissertation, University of Illinois at Urbana-Champaign, 1977. Several recordings of African-American Sacred Harp singing are commercially available including: Kathryn King, producer, *The Colored Sacred Harp*: Wiregrass Sacred Harp Singers, New World Records, 1993; and Henry Willett, producer, *Wiregrass Notes: Black Sacred Harp Singing from Southeast Alabama*, Alabama Traditions, 1982.

The Deasons: A Christian Harmony Family

[1] William Walker, *The Christian Harmony*, (Alabama Christian Harmony Publishing Company, revised 1994).

[2] William Walker, *The Christian Harmony*, Revised by John Deason and O.A. Parris (Christian Harmony Publishing Company, 1958), p.135.

[3] *Ibid.*, p.21.

[4] *Ibid.*, p. 273.

[5] *Ibid.*, pp. 289, 287.

[6] Deason, Henry H., *Deason Family News*, Issue No. 2, (Jan 1995), p. 1.

[7] James Scholten, "William Walker's *Christian Harmony* in Alabama: A Study of the Tunebook and Its Traditions," (unpublished) Ohio University, 1980, pp. 8-12.

[8] Walker's brother-in-law, B.F. White, subscribed to the four-shape notation system in his book *The Sacred Harp*, another important songbook with a strong following in the South. While there was a sense of rivalry at one time between four-shape singers and seven-shape singers, according to Art Deason, they now appreciate and support each other and often sing together. In fact, in the 1980s Deason worked with the State Arts Council to organize an annual Capitol City Shape Note Singing, which brings singers together from the four shape-note hymnals published in Alabama: the Cooper *Sacred Harp*, the Denson *Sacred Harp*, the Jackson *Colored Sacred Harp*, and the *Christian Harmony*. In the *National Sacred Harp Newsletter*, Deason commented, "There's just something special about singers who sing and promote their own

publisher's books, but who are willing to come together to help create and maintain the old tradition of shape note singing. Such cooperative spirit gives everybody the opportunity to sing together in all shape note books present. One brother remarked, 'When we get to heaven, there will not be any brand name song books such as *Christian Harmony* and *Sacred Harp*. We will all be as one.'"

9 James Scholten, p.19.

(A continuous tradition of singings from the various editions of the *Christian Harmony* exist elsewhere in the South, mainly in North and South Carolina, and north and west central Alabama.)

[10]Art Deason, author interview, September 30, 1994.

[11]James Scholten, pp. 23-25.

[12]Art Deason, author interview, September 30, 1994.

[13]William Walker, *The Christian Harmony*, (Alabama Christian Harmony Singing Association, Inc., rev. 1994), pp. v-xx.

[14]James Scholten, pp. 30-31.

[15]Deason, Art, "Shape Notables," *Shape Notes*, Vol. VII, No. 1, (January-February 1995), p. 3.

[16]*Ibid.*, p. 3.

[17]Art Deason, author interview, September 30, 1994.

[18]Art Deason, author interview, September 30, 1994.

Community and the Jefferson County . . .

The following taped interviews were cited or consulted. The interviews were conducted by the author, unless otherwise indicated.

JAMES ALLEN: late 1978.

CHARLES BRIDGES: November 24, 1978; January 1981 (conducted by Ray Funk).

TOM LACEY and SAM MIDDLEBROOKS: Late 1978; August 19, 1979.

TOM LACEY: February 5, 1979; October 23, 1981; August 1, 1983; August 2, 1983 (conducted by Lynn Abbott); November 28, 1983; January 9, 1984; and January 19, 1984.

AULSTON MOULTON: October 8, 1979.

SOLLIE J. PUGH: Late 1978; February 6, 1979; July 25, 1980.

Special thanks to Lynn Abbott.

Reading and Listening

ABBOTT, LYNN. **Monograph**, "The Soproco Spiritual Singers: A New Orleans Quartet Family Tree" (published by Jean Lafitte National Historical Park, 1983). **Liner notes**, "Religious Recordings From Black New Orleans: 1924-1931" (504 Records LP20, 1989). Mr. Abbott details the spread of the "Birmingham quartet training culture" to New Orleans in the early 1930s, carried by Gilbert Porterfield and Sandy Newell, former members of the Bessemer Red Rose Quartet. Mr. Porterfield was a quartet trainer of very high stature.

CAUTHEN,JOYCE. **Liner notes**, "John Alexander's Sterling Jubilee Singers of Bessemer, Alabama" (Alabama Traditions 105, 1994).

DIXON, R.M.W. & GODRICH, J. *Blues & Gospel Records 1902-1943*. Storyville Publications, Essex, England, 1982.

McCALLUM, BRENDA. **Liner notes**, "The Birmingham Boys," Alabama Traditions 101 (1982). Includes essays and commentary by Brenda McCallum, Ray Funk and Clarence Horace Boyer. The products of the late Brenda McCallum's two years research on Jefferson County gospel quartet traditions are housed at the Archive of American Minority Cultures at the University of Alabama in Tuscaloosa, where she served as director.

SEROFF, DOUG. **Book chapter**, "On The Battlefield: Gospel Quartets in Jefferson County, Alabama, in *Repercussions*, ed. Geoffrey Haydon and Dennis Marks (Century Publishing, London, 1985, pp. 30-54). **Essay**, "African-American Gospel Singing Traditions," in *Musical Roots of the South*, ed. Peggy Bulger (booklet published by the Southern Arts Federation, 1991). **Essay**, "Gospel Quartet Singing," in *Alabama Folklife*: *Collected Essays*," ed. Steve Martin (Alabama Folklife Association, 1989). **Liner notes**, "Birmingham Quartet Anthology," (Clanka Lanka 144,001/ 002, Sweden, 1980). **Liner notes**, "The Four Eagles Gospel Singers" (Global Village C277, 1992). **Program booklet**, "Birmingham Quartet Scrapbook; A Quartet Reunion in Jefferson County." (Publication funded by the National Endowment for the Arts, 1980). **Essay**, "A Legacy of Music Education," in "Gospel Arts Day Nashville." (Program booklet funded by the National Endowment for the Arts, 1988). **Essay**, "How Shall We Sing The Lord's Song In A Foreign Land?" in "Gospel Arts Day Nashville." (Program booklet funded by the National Endowment for the Arts, 1989). **Program booklet**, "Home Of The Heroes." (Publication funded by the National Endowment for the Arts, 1990). **Essay**, "Black American Quartet Traditions," in "Smithsonian Performing Arts Program in Black American Culture." (Program booklet published by Smithsonian Performing Arts, 1981). **Essays** which appear in *Repercussions*, the "Gospel Arts Day Nashville" publications, the "Home Of The Heroes" program booklet, and the Smithsonian Performing Arts program booklet attempt to place the Jefferson County quartet phenomenon in a broader historical context, including a discussion of the important influence of Bessemer quartet trainer Norman McQueen in Chicago.

"Birmingham Quartet Anthology" (Clanka Lanka 144,001/002 Sweden, 1980). A 2-LP set, with booklet notes. Includes thirty-two historic recordings of Jefferson County, Alabama gospel quartets, originally recorded 1926-1953. Artists include the Birmingham Jubilee Singers, Dunham Jubilee Singers, Famous Blue Jay Singers, others. Nominated for Grammy Award as "Best Historical Album" in 1981. This set is currently out-of-print.

"Birmingham Boys" (Alabama Traditions 101. Funded by the National Endowment for the Arts, 1982). Jefferson County male quartets, including the Sterling Jubilee Singers, recorded 1980-1981. Includes booklet notes.

Birmingham Sunlights—"For Old Time's Sake" (Flying Fish FF90588, 1992). The youngest and most recent off-spring of the Jefferson County gospel quartet heritage, the Birmingham Sunlights received training from the Sterling Jubilee Singers and other area quartets.

"Four Eagles Gospel-Singers" (Global Village C227, 1992). One of Jefferson County's premier traditional gospel quartets, the Four Eagles celebrated their 56th Anniversary in November 1994.

"John Alexander's Sterling Jubilee Singers" (Alabama Traditions 105, 1994). Unissued Field Recordings, featuring many of the area's traditional gospel groups are part of the collection at the Center for Popular Music, Middle Tennessee State University, Murfreesboro, TN. These recordings were collected over the past five years by recording engineer Bruce Nemerov.

OTHER RESOURCES

Film Documentary, "On The Battlefield — Gospel Quartets in Jefferson County, Alabama," part of the *Repercussions* film series, for RM Arts and Channel Four Television, Great Britain (Third Eye Productions, Geoffrey Haydon, director, 1984).

This one-hour documentary features the Sterling Jubilees, Four Eagles, Birmingham Sunlights and other traditional gospel quartets in performance, rehearsal and a training session. Doug Seroff was consultant. Video copies are commercially available through Original Music, Tivoli, New York.

Sand Mountain's Wootten Family: Sacred Harp Singers

[1] A recording from one of the Woottens' annual singing sessions has been commercially available, and another is being readied. Inquiries can be sent to Hollow Square Productions, 2216 Shady Dell Lane, Birmingham, AL 35216.

[2] "All-Day Singing" (New York), p. 51.

Suggested Readings on Sacred Harp Singing

Cobb, Buell E., Jr. *The Sacred Harp: A Tradition and Its Music.* Athens: University of Georgia Press, 1978, 1989.

Jackson, George Pullen. *White Spirituals in the Southern Uplands.* Chapel Hill: University of North Carolina Press, 1933, 1965.

Seven-shape-note Gospel Music in Northern Alabama

Much of the background for this essay is drawn from a book in progress about the history of southern gospel music. Several specific sources, however, relate to the Athens Music Company and the personalities involved. These include personal interviews with Jake Williams, Bill Harrison, Dwight Brock, Jake Hess, Lionel Delmore, Connor Hall, and Otis McCoy. A general, albeit brief, overview of southern gospel history is found in my entry on the subject in *The Encyclopedia of Southern Culture* (Chapel Hill: UNC Press, 1989, 1013, 1014). Other writings include a history of quartet development I published in *Folk Music and Modern Sound*, ed. William Ferris and Mary Hart (U Press of Mississippi, 1982). Other general histories of gospel include Lois Blackwell, *The Wings of a Dove* (1978), and Bob Terrell's *The Music Men: The Story of Professional Gospel Quartet Singing* (self-published, 1990).

Sources for biographical data include the author's own files, as well as Ottis J. Knippers *Who's Who Among Southern Singers and Composers* (Lawrenceburg: James D. Vaughan, 1937) and Clarice Baxter and Videt Polk, *Gospel Song Writers Biography* (Dallas: Stamps-Baxter, 1971). Information about G.T. Speer and his family can be found in Paula Becker, *Let the Song Go On: Fifty Years of Gospel Singing with the Speer Family* (Nashville: Impact Books, 1971). Quotations from Alton Delmore come from his *Truth Is Stranger Than Publicity*, ed. by Charles Wolfe (Nashville: Country Music Foundation Press, 1977) — a new, revised edition is currently in press. For information about Elvis Presley and Jake Hess, see Charles Wolfe, "Elvis and the Gospel Tradition," in *The Elvis Reader* (New York: St. Martin's Press, 1992), as well as the annotations book for the CD set *Elvis Presley: Amazing Grace: His Greatest Sacred Performances* (RCA 66421-2), also by Charles Wolfe.

Cry Holy Unto the Lord

[1] Personal interview with the author, October 24, 1988.

[2] Howard Wight Marshall, "Keep on the Sunny Side': Pattern and Religious Expression in Bluegrass Gospel Music." *New York Folklore Quarterly* 39(1): 3-43. 1974.

[3] Donald G. Matthews, Religion in the Old South. Chicago: The University of Chicago Press. 1977.

[4] Bill Monroe, cited in Thomas Goldsmith, Liner notes to Bill Monroe and His Blue Grass Boys, "Crying Holy Unto the Lord." MCA Records (MCAC 10017). 1991.

[5] Bill Monroe, cited in Alice (Gerrard) Foster and Ralph Rinzler, Liner notes to Bill Monroe and His Blue Grass Boys, "A Voice From on High." Decca Records (DL 75135). 1969.

[6] Personal interview with the author, May 30, 1994.

ADDITIONAL READING

Cantwell, Robert. *Bluegrass Breakdown: The Making of the Old Southern Sound*. Urbana: University of Illinois Press. 1984.

Heilbut, Anthony. *The Gospel Sound: Good News and Bad Times*. New York: Limelight Editions. 1985.

Levine, Lawrence W. *Black Culture and Black Consciousness: Afro-American Folk Thought from Slavery to Freedom*, pp. 136-189: "Freedom, Culture, and Religion." Oxford: Oxford University Press. 1977.

Nash, Alanna. "Bill Monroe." Interview in: Alanna Nash, *Behind Closed Doors: Talking with the Legends of Country Music*, pp. 327-354. New York: Alfred A. Knopf. 1988.

Rinzler, Ralph. "Bill Monroe." In: Bill C. Malone and Judith McCulloh, eds., *Stars of Country Music: Uncle Dave Macon to Johnny Rodriguez*, pp. 202-221. Urbana: University of Illinois Press. 1975.

Rosenberg, Neil V. *Bluegrass: A History*. Urbana: University of Illinois Press. 1985.

Synan, Vinson. *The Holiness-Pentecostal Movement in the United States*. Grand Rapids: William B. Eerdmans Publishing Co. 1971.

RECOMMENDED LISTENING

Lester Flatt and Earl Scruggs and the Foggy Mountain Boys, "You Can Feel It In Your Soul" (County CCS 111).

The Louvin Brothers, "Radio Favorites '51-'57" (Country Music Foundation CMF-009D).

The Louvin Brothers, "The Louvin Brothers" (Rounder Records Special Series 07).

The Monroe Brothers, "Feast Here Tonight" (RCA Bluebird AMX2-5510).

Bill Monroe and His Blue Grass Boys, "A Voice From On High" (Decca DL 75135).

Bill Monroe, "The Music of Bill Monroe from 1936 to 1994" (MCA MCAD4-11048).

Bill Monroe and His Blue Grass Boys, "The Essential Bill Monroe and His Blue Grass Boys, 1945-1949" (Columbia/Legacy C2K 52478).

Claire Lynch, "Friends for a Lifetime" (Brentwood CD-5362J).

The Sullivan Family. Several cassette recordings are available by mail from the Sullivans. Write: Box 69, St. Stephens, AL 37343, (334) 246-0717.

Jerry and Tammy Sullivan, "A Joyful Noise" (Country Music Foundation CMF-016D).

About the Authors

Jack Bernhardt has written extensively on bluegrass and country music. He serves as Traditional and Country Music critic for the Raleigh, North Carolina *News and Observer* and runs his own public relations consulting firm. He earned his M.A. in Folklore at the University of North Carolina at Chapel Hill and his M.A. in Anthropology at Kent State University.

Joyce Cauthen is an independent music scholar and festival producer and serves as president of the Alabama Folklife Association. She is the author of *With Fiddle and Well-Rosined Bow: Old-Time Fiddling in Alabama*, and has produced several documentary recordings including *Possum Up A Gum Stump: Commercial and Field Recordings of Alabama Fiddlers* and *John Alexander's Sterling Jubilee Singers of Bessemer, Alabama*. She earned her MA in English at Purdue University.

Buell Cobb is the author of *The Sacred Harp: A Tradition and Its Music* and is an active Sacred Harp singer. He has written articles on the Sacred Harp tradition for *Southern Exposure, Virginia Quarterly Review* and *Louisiana Studies,* and is the co-producer of the audio-cassette *Bound for Canaan: Sacred Harp Singing from Sand Mountain, Alabama.*

Willie Collins earned his Ph.D. in Ethnomusicology at the University of California at Los Angeles. His dissertation topic was "The Moan-and-Prayer Event in Two African-American Churches in Southeast Alabama." He has served as city folklorist in Los Angeles and Oakland, California, and is a former faculty member at Tuskegee University.

Fred C. Fussell is director of the Chattahoochee Valley Folklife Project. As chief curator at the Columbus (Georgia) Museum, Fussell curated numerous folklife exhibits and served as the director of the Chattahoochee Folk Festival. He produced a two-volume recorded anthology of regional music, *In Celebration of a Legacy: The Traditional Music of the Chattahoochee Valley.*

Erin Kellen is director of the Sacred Harp Video Project, an initiative of the Alabama Center for Traditional Culture. Her folklife research in

Alabama's Piney Woods has focused on Margie Sullivan, bluegrass gospel performer, and the role of women in early bluegrass music. She has, in the past, worked at the Alabama Center for Traditional Culture and the Southern Folklife Collection at the University of North Carolina at Chapel Hill.

Anne H.F. Kimzey is Folklife Specialist with the Alabama Center for Traditional Culture. In her work at the Center she has served as producer of the Alabama Folkways Radio Series, portions of which have aired on National Public Radio. Her radio production work has led her to research a number of Alabama's sacred music traditions.

Doug Seroff has independently researched African-American vocal harmony traditions and black music history for nearly twenty years. He has co-produced two videodocumentaries on gospel quartet singing and produced the LP record *Birmingham Quartet Anthology,* which was nominated for a Grammy Award in 1980. He has produced concert events and written numerous articles on Birmingham's gospel quartet tradition.

Henry Willett, Director of the Alabama Center for Traditional Culture, has been researching the state's folk traditions for nearly twenty years. He is founder of the Alabama Folklife Association, has produced films, recordings, exhibits and festivals and has published numerous articles on Alabama folklife, including the state's sacred music traditions. He earned his M.A. in Folk Studies from Western Kentucky University. He formerly served as Regional Representative to the Southern States for the National Endowment for the Arts and as Assistant Director of the Alabama State Council on the Arts.

Charles Wolfe is one of the world's leading authorities on southern traditional and country music. He is the author of eight books and dozens of articles on the subject, and has received three Grammy nominations for annotating and producing traditional music recordings. He earned his M.A. and Ph.D. in English at the University of Kansas and serves on the faculty at Middle Tennessee State University. He is currently completing a history of southern gospel music for the University of Illinois Press.

PLAYLIST

1. Wootten Family, "Ragan"

2. Wootten Family, "King of Peace"

3. Sullivan Family, "No More Dying"

4. Reformed Presbyterian Church of Selma, "Crimond"

5. Reformed Presbyterian Church of Selma, "Azmon"

6. Ramah Baptist Church, "I Heard the Voice of Jesus Say, Come Unto Me and Rest"

7. Judge Jackson, "Glory Shone Around"

8. Donald Smith and Doug Wyers, "Mercy Seat"

9. Deason Family, "Raymond"

10. Mt. Pleasant Primitive Baptist Church, "Beside the Gospel Pool, Appointed For the Poor"

11. Brown's Ferry Four, "Bound for the Shore"

12. North Alabama Singing Convention, "He's My Help In Time of Need"

13. Big Four Singers of Bessemer, "Golden Bells"

14. Spring Hill Baptist Church, "Moaning"

15. Jerry and Tammy Sullivan, "When Jesus Passed By"

A Division of the
Alabama State Council on the Arts